LASER
50 YEARS OF
DISCOVERIES

LASER
50 YEARS OF
DISCOVERIES

Fabien Bretenaker
Laboratoire Aimé Cotton, France

Nicolas Treps
University Pierre and Marie Curie, France

Published by

World Scientific Publishing Co. Pte. Ltd.
5 Toh Tuck Link, Singapore 596224
USA office: 27 Warren Street, Suite 401-402, Hackensack, NJ 07601
UK office: 57 Shelton Street, Covent Garden, London WC2H 9HE

Library of Congress Cataloging-in-Publication Data
Bretenaker, Fabien, 1966–   author.
    Laser : 50 years of discoveries / Fabien Bretenaker (Laboratoire Aimé Cotton, France),
Nicolas Treps (University Pierre and Marie Curie, France).
    pages cm
    ISBN 978-9814612401 (hardcover : alk. paper)
    ISBN 978-9814641968 (softcover : alk. paper)
    1. Lasers. I. Treps, Nicolas, author. II. Title.
    TA1675.B73 2014
    621.36'6--dc23
                                            2014018320

British Library Cataloguing-in-Publication Data
A catalogue record for this book is available from the British Library.

Originally published in French as "**Le Laser**" by EDP Sciences.
Copyright © EDP Sciences 2010. A co-publication with EDP Sciences, 17, rue du Hoggar, Parc
d'activités de Courtaboeuf BP 112, 91944 Les Ulis Cedex A, France.

This edition is distributed worldwide by World Scientific Publishing Co. Pte. ltd., except France.

Copyright © 2015 by World Scientific Publishing Co. Pte. Ltd.

In-house Editor: Song Yu

Typeset by Stallion Press
Email: enquiries@stallionpress.com

Preface

Fifty years after their invention, lasers continue to amaze us. Their performance characteristics are constantly reaching new limits, and the scope of their applications continues to expand. Perhaps the best measure of the success of the technology is that we in fact forget that lasers are present in many different facets of our daily lives. Yet it took years of effort by teams of physicists to transform the fundamental notions of Einstein into the first experimental beam of laser light generated in a ruby crystal. Since these pioneering studies, lasers of all sorts and sizes have been developed.

Without having the ambition to cover all applications that have now become numerous in both scientific laboratories and in industry, this book provides an overview (from many writers and different perspectives) of various aspects of science and technology that have developed as a result of the laser's invention. The foreword is written by Charles Townes, one of the inventors of the laser, and 1964 Nobel Laureate in physics. His reflections vividly trace the little known and sometimes amusing history of the pioneering discovery that has revolutionized the panoramas of science and industry for over half a century. After presentation of the principles of laser operation, each chapter then describes different types of laser sources (from the largest to smallest) as well as their applications. Long considered a laboratory curiosity ("a solution in search of a problem"), lasers have now become central in many areas of fundamental research and industry. This is an important lesson for the future.

Lasers first become indispensable in the field of metrology: telemetry to measure distances, vibrometry for testing solid structures; the use of gyroscopes for aircraft, ships and spacecraft etc. Lidar technology today brings us security and improved quality of life through improved air transport safety and the detection of air pollution. Lasers have rapidly become essential tools in areas such as medicine, chemistry, and mechanical engineering. The industry of machine tooling has been revolutionized by the development of powerful lasers for welding, cutting, soldering, and marking.

For the general public, the incredible emergence of lasers in practical life has arisen with the advent of semiconductor lasers (the size of a pinhead!), CDs and DVDs that allow massive information storage, and the Internet where information coded on laser light is propagated globally through optical fibers to shape daily life of the modern world.

Lasers have also enabled spectacular advances in basic research: quantum optics, potential detection of gravitational wave, tests of general relativity and theories of cosmology. Research over the past 30 years on "cold atoms" is leading to important applications for space navigation. And we are also very far from completing the basic research in laser sources themselves, constantly pushing the limits of technology to new frontiers. Ultraviolet and X-ray lasers are only in their infancy, and at the other end of the spectrum, terahertz lasers are seeing spectacular growth and should find many applications in chemistry and in the field of detection and security. The development of very high power "extreme light" lasers is a field of research very active internationally, for both fundamental tests of basic physics as well as for an important test of models and simulations. On the horizon for tomorrow are many new applications of lasers in medicine, such as the treatment of macular degeneration of the eye, an affliction affecting tens of millions of people worldwide.

The laser clearly has a very bright and unexplored future ahead of it. The content of this book has been written by leading researchers involved in the development and applications of lasers, with the authors and their affiliations given at the beginning of each chapter. Putting this book together has been coordinated by two brilliant young researchers Fabien Bretenaker and Nicolas Treps. This book is destined for all who are curious about science and technology. It is particularly aimed at those at high school, their teachers as well as science students at all levels. The book covers a wide variety of topics, all treated as simply as possible and in a way that is clear and easy to follow. There are many figures and diagrams and very few equations.

The publication of this book in English is particularly appropriate to celebrate the International Year of Light and Light-based Technologies in 2015, where the United Nations General Assembly has recognized the importance of both fundamental and applied research in lasers and their applications. This year will allow a truly global appreciation of the many ways in which the laser has played a central role in modern life, and how it will be a central tool to develop solutions for challenges of the future in healthcare, communications and quality of life worldwide.

Michèle Leduc
President of the
Fédération Française
des Sociétés Scientifiques

John Dudley
President of the
European Physical Society

Michèle Leduc

John Dudley

Michèle Leduc is senior researcher at Laboratoire Kastler Brossel in Ecole Normale Supérieure in Paris, France. She heads the Institut Francilien de Recherche sur les Atomes Froids (IFRAF).

John Dudley is Professor of Physics at University of Franche-Comté and CNRS Institute FEMTO-ST in Besançon, France, and President of the European Physical Society (2013–2015).

Coordinators, Contributors, and Acknowledgments

This collective book has been written by 15 co-authors whose names are reproduced at the beginning of each chapter and below. The coordination has been performed by Fabien Bretenaker and Nicolas Treps, with the complicity of Michèle Leduc and Michel Le Bellac.

Fabien Bretenaker   Nicolas Treps

Fabien Bretenaker is senior scientist at CNRS. He graduated from Ecole Polytechnique in 1988 and received in 1992 the PhD degree from University of Rennes, France, after having worked on ring lasers and their applications to rotation sensing. He worked during some years for Sagem company and joined CNRS in 1994, first in the laser physics lab in Rennes. In 2003, he joined Laboratoire Aimé Cotton in Orsay, France. He is also professor at Ecole Polytechnique. His research deals with laser physics, nonlinear optics, quantum optics, with applications ranging from microwave photonics to sensors.

Nicolas Treps is professor at university Pierre and Marie Curie in Paris, France. He graduated from Ecole Polytechnique and received the PhD degree in 2001 after his work on quantum properties of optical images in Laboratoire Kastler-Brossel. He was then a post-doctoral researcher at Australian National University in Canberra, during which he worked on quantum information protocols. Since 2002, he has been working in Laboratoire Kastler-Brossel. His research covers the fields of quantum aspects of light, high sensitivity measurements, nonlinear optics, and quantum information science.

Contributors

The following people have contributed to the writing of this book: Mehdi Alouini, Philippe Balcou, Claude Boccara, Christian Chardonnet, Pierre-François Cohadon, Nicolas Forget, Sébastien Forget, Saïda Guelatti-Khélifa, Manuel Joffre, Lucile Julien, Michèle Leduc, Serge Mordon, Isabelle Robert-Philip, Thierry Ruchon, and Catherine Schwob. We warmly thank them for their work and the friendly atmosphere which has governed our collaboration.

Acknowledgments

We wish to express our special thanks to Michèle Leduc who has trusted us enough to ask us to coordinated this book, for her warm friendship, her permanent enthusiasm and her instrumental help. We also thank Michel Le Bellac for his help with the translation, his advices, his critical reading of the entire book and his incredible experience when it comes to writing physics books. We warmly thank Charles Townes for having provided us with his memories in the foreword of this book. We also thank John Dudley for having co-written the preface of this book.

The authors of this book have received the help from many people. In particular, we wish to thank Diane Morel, Benoit Appert-Collin, Alexios Beveratos, Amit Raj Dhawan, Jean-Pierre Cariou, Anthony Carré, Jean-Pierre Chièze, France Citrini, Jean Fontanieu, Guillaume Gorju, Sinan Haliyo, Vincent Josse, John Lopez, Philippe Nicolaï, Daniel Rugar, Laurent Sauvage, Guy Schurtz, Sylvain Schwartz, and Pierre Verlot. Finally, the final achievement of this book has been made possible thanks to the warm hospitality of Rupamanjari Ghosh and Amrita Madan.

Foreword

Charles H. Townes

Professor at University of California, Berkeley

The physical principles by which lasers operate were known quite early in the 20th century; in 1924 Richard Tolman wrote "Molecules in the upper quantum state may return to the lower quantum state in such a way as to reinforce the primary beam by negative absorption — it will be pointed out that for absorption experiments as usually performed the amount of negative absorption can be neglected".[1] But it was about 30 years later before the usefulness of amplification by "negative absorption" was really recognized. Furthermore, lasers and many masers have existed around particular stars for billions of years. If we had taken the trouble some time ago to look systematically in the microwave range, we would have found the intense microwave radiation from masers around stars, probably figured out how this radiation was produced, and initiated the field of masers and lasers earlier.

In the 1950s, I was doing microwave spectroscopy on molecules using electronic oscillators. This provided very high spectral resolution, but such oscillators could not produce wavelengths shorter than a few millimeters and I was eager to get to shorter wavelengths — into the infrared, because of the wealth of interesting spectra there. After some unsuccessful work in this direction, I was asked to chair a national committee to investigate such possibilities. We visited many laboratories and had much discussion, but found no solution. Before the committee's last meeting, I woke up

---

[1] Richard Tolman, *Phys. Rev.* **24**, 297 (1924).

early in the morning worrying about our lack of success. It was a bright morning, and I went outside to sit on a park bench. I thought that of course, molecules and atoms can produce short wavelengths, but I had previously ruled out their use because thermodynamics limits the intensity of radiation to an amount determined by their temperature. Suddenly I woke up to the fact that molecules and atoms do not have to obey thermodynamics; we can put more in the upper than in the lower state. Since I was then at Columbia University where much work was being done with molecular and atomic beams to separate their different states, I thought of using this technique. Pulling out paper and pencil from my pockets, I wrote down appropriate equations and numbers. It looked like it could work!

On returning to Columbia I persuaded a graduate student, Jim Gordon, to try to build such a system for amplification. Since I had much microwave equipment and was very familiar with the microwave spectra of molecules, I thought we should try it first with beams of ammonia molecules, to amplify and produce an oscillator at about 1 cm wavelength. After Gordon, with the help of a post doc Herb Zeiger, had worked a couple of years on building such a system, Prof Kusch, chairman of the physics department, and Prof. Rabi, the previous chairman of the department, came into my lab saying "Charlie, that's not going to work, and you know it won't work. You're wasting the department's money, and must stop". I disagreed, and they left my lab annoyed. About two months later, in April, 1954, Jim Gordon came into the seminar where I was teaching, and announced "It's working". We all left the class and went to the lab to see this new oscillator. Kusch and Rabi were both specialists in molecular beams and both won Nobel Prizes. This shows it is not just intelligence that produces new results. We must leave the known routes and take chances.

Although it turned out that Basov and Prokhorov in the Soviet Union had an idea somewhat similar to mine, we were not in contact until after our system was working (theirs was not yet). Many Americans and some Europeans had visited my lab and seen our experiment underway, but were doubtful and hence not interested. And no one I knew was interested or optimistic enough to compete with our work.

My students and I, one day at lunch, had picked out the name "maser" for the new device, the acronym for "microwave amplification by stimulated emission of radiation". After we announced operation of the new amplifier, many people became interested. It became a hot field with much competition.

I continued work on masers, but soon went to the Ecole Normale Supérieure in Paris on sabbatical leave. There I worked in Alfred Kastler's lab, where Claude Cohen-Tannoudji, then a student, Jean Combrisson, and Arnold Honig, one of my former students, were all busy with research. The latter two were working on electron spin resonances in semiconductors, and had just discovered long relaxation times of electron spin excitation. Wow! That meant that electron spins could be in the excited state for some time, and tunable masers could be made, on which we published. This is an example of the importance of interaction of scientists in different fields, which often produces new ideas.

In Europe, I met Niels Bohr and while walking on the street with him he asked what I was working on. I told him about the ammonia maser, and the very pure frequency of oscillation it produced. "Oh no, that can't be right", he said. "You must misunderstand". I explained to him that yes, we had measured it and this was true, but we parted without his ever believing it. He must have been thinking of the uncertainty principle, and not allowing for averaging over a large number of molecules. But this illustrates how even the greatest often get locked into their own fixed ideas, and don't see new ones.

The maser became a very hot field. But I was, of course, interested in getting to shorter wavelengths. Almost everyone thought there was no chance of producing much shorter waves, but after a couple of years with the maser I decided I must see how best to get on to shorter waves, and I took some time to think more about it. This led me to recognize, and show numerically, that we could make "masers" that operated right on down to optical wavelengths. But I decided to keep quiet about it until I worked it all out, because the field was then exciting and I knew someone would compete and try to publish the first paper once they recognized this possibility. I was consulting at Bell Labs, where my former post doc, Art Schawlow, who became my brother-in-law by marrying my kid sister, was then working. I mentioned my idea and the possibility of getting down to light waves. He responded "Oh, I've been wondering about that — could be work together on it". I said "sure", and we did. He added the important idea of two parallel plates as a resonator (he had done spectroscopy with a Fabry–Perot, which probably gave him the idea). This was an important improvement over my plan to use simply a closed cavity, as I had done at microwave frequencies. We decided to first publish a theoretical paper before doing experiments, since once anyone recognized the possibility, they were likely to compete and try to publish before us. So we published such a paper.

Before publication, Schawlow and I decided it appropriate to give the patent on "optical masers" to Bell Labs, and he took it to their patent lawyers. He telephoned me a few days later. Bell Labs' patent lawyers had said light was of no value to communications, and hence they were not interested and we could patent it ourselves if we wished. We knew they were wrong — another example of the turndown of new ideas by experienced people — and I asked him to go back to persuade them it could be used for communications. They then agreed to write a patent, which we labeled "Optical Masers and Communication".

Schawlow and I wrote and published the paper "Optical Masers" to establish the field before trying to build one. The natural name "Laser" for Light Amplification by Stimulated Emission of Radiation came along a little later. With this publication, many people began to try to build a laser, including students in my lab. However, at that time I was asked to go to Washington and take an important position in advising the government, which I agreed to do. This gave me little time to help my students build the first laser, and they didn't.

Ted Maiman produced the first laser in May, 1960, using a ruby crystal and an intense light flash. The latter was a great idea to provide at least temporary excitation, and I had not thought of it. Maiman succeeded, and produced a great flash — not only of red light, but also in the public press! It was the first operating laser. A number were subsequently produced. The next new lasers were made by Mirek Stevenson and Peter Sorokin at General Electric, and then the helium–neon gas laser by Ali Javan, one of my former students, along with Bill Bennett and Don Herriott, at Bell Labs. All of the inventors of the early lasers had recently been students at universities working in fields related to spectroscopy, and all of the inventions were in industrial laboratories. Industry had become interested, could work fast, and was very successful!

Many people, engineers and scientists, have contributed to the rapid growth and enormous usefulness of lasers. It has transformed the field of optics. It is important in many fields, a number of which were not envisioned during the initiation of the laser. I did not, for example, foresee any medical usages. But now that is a big and important application. Nonlinear optics is one of the many new creations. And still shorter laser waves which were not initially foreseen — X-rays and gamma-rays — have become interesting. No new acronyms, such as xasers for X-rays have been introduced — devices are lasers at every wavelength except for microwaves. The latter are still masers even though there is no distinction between masers and lasers except that the name maser is for wavelengths above about 1 millimeter.

I was initially especially interested in scientific uses of the new device, and am delighted to see all the new science produced. I'm now using lasers to measure the sizes and shapes of stars. More than a dozen Nobel Prizes have been awarded to scientists who used masers or lasers as critical instruments in their work. Penzias and Wilson used a maser amplifier in discovery the "big bang" origin of the universe.

Technical applications of lasers have, of course, made an even bigger impact on our society and on economics than the pure science applications. The laser industry now involves many, many billions of dollars per year, and can be expected to continue to grow rapidly.

The laser is a classic example of how fundamental research contributes not only to science, but also, enormously, many times completely unexpectedly, to economics. Basic science is fascinating, and also is likely to help human welfare enormously. The interesting chapters of this book will provide some examples.

Table of Contents

Chapter 1

What is a Laser?

Lucile Julien

Professor, Université Pierre et Marie Curie,
Laboratoire Kastler Brossel, Paris, France

Catherine Schwob

Professor, Université Pierre et Marie Curie,
Institut des NanoSciences de Paris, Paris, France

The first laser was built more than 50 years ago, in May 1960: it was a pulsed ruby laser. It was a simple laboratory curiosity and nobody knew what its usefulness could be. Other devices were rapidly demonstrated, and the variety and number of lasers in the world increased at a huge rate. Currently, the annual laser world market is worth about 6 billion dollars. Thanks to the remarkable properties of laser light, laser applications increase steadily in the domains of industry, building, medicine, telecommunications, etc. One can find many lasers in research laboratories, and they are used more and more in our everyday life and almost everybody has already seen a laser beam. The goal of the first chapter of this book is to explain simply what a laser is, how it is built and how it operates. Firstly, let us point out the outstanding properties of the laser light.

1.1. A Device Which Provides a Quite Distinctive Beam

1.1.1. *The laser beam*

A laser beam can be recognized at first glance since it differs from ordinary light. Physicists say that it is a beam of coherent light. We will see here that its properties are different from those of light emitted by ordinary lamps, that we will call "classical lamps" in the following. Such lamps are

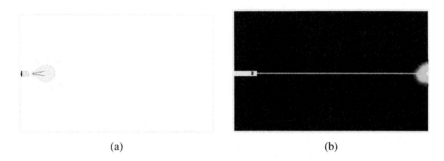

(a)   (b)

Figure 1.1:   The light emitted by a classical lamp (a) enlightens in all directions; the laser (b) emits a narrow beam in a given direction.

of different types: incandescent light bulbs, tube lights, and light-emitting diodes. But they all emit light in all directions, which is convenient to light up a room or a given space, as shown in Figure 1.1. On the contrary, a laser emits a narrow beam giving a localized light spot when something like a wall gets in its way.

Even if the laser beam propagates over large distances, it remains parallel and well-defined. This property is called spatial coherence. Another property of a laser beam, in the visible domain, is its color, which is often pure, that means not superimposed to other colors. This second property is called monochromaticity or temporal coherence.

We can then give a first answer to the question "What is a laser?": A laser is a device which delivers coherent light (both spatially and temporally). Let us see now how this light is generated; we begin by recalling the physical nature of light.

1.1.2.   *What is the nature of light?*

Light is an electromagnetic wave, which means electric and magnetic fields coupled together and propagating in space, the combination of both being called an electromagnetic field. Since the 19th century, it has been known that a varying electric field induces a magnetic field and, in the same manner, a varying magnetic field induces an electric field. The coupling of these two fields with each other, and with electric charges and currents, are described by Maxwell's equations (1831–1879) which give the behavior of an electromagnetic field and the way it propagates. In an electromagnetic wave, both fields oscillate at the same frequency, that is, their number of oscillations per second, and propagate together in vacuum at the velocity c, known as the *velocity of light*.

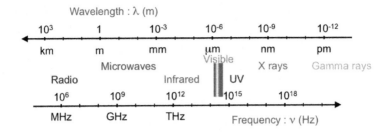

Figure 1.2: The various domains covered by electromagnetic waves.

The velocity of light is a universal constant. From the theory of relativity, developed by Einstein in 1905, we know that this velocity is the same for all observers. Due to the new definition of the meter in 1983, it has now a fixed value in the international system of units, given by 299,972,458 m/s, which is about 300,000 km/s.

Light is an electromagnetic wave, but the domain of electromagnetic waves is much wider than visible light. It spreads over a large frequency domain, shown in Figure 1.2, from radiofrequency waves in the low frequency range to gamma rays in the high frequency one. The optical domain lies in the middle of this spectrum, with the visible range surrounded by infrared on the one side and ultraviolet on the other.

Each frequency is related to a wavelength, given by $\lambda = \frac{c}{\nu}$. Large wavelengths are then associated with low frequencies and small ones to high frequencies. In the visible domain, the wavelengths range from 400 to 800 nm (1 nm = 10^{-9} m that is 1 billionth of meter). In this domain, our eye associates a color to a group of wavelengths: violet, blue, green, yellow, orange, red, in order of increasing wavelengths. These rainbow colors are those obtained when white light is dispersed by a prism or a drop of water.

At the center of the visible spectrum, the wavelength is 600 nm and the frequency 500 THz, that is 500,000 billion oscillations per second (1 THz = 10^{12} Hz). Frequency is the inverse of time (1 Hz = 1 s^{-1}); that is why monochromaticity mentioned above is called a *temporal* property of light.

1.1.3. *Photons different from others*

During the 20th century, quantum mechanics has deeply changed the way we describe the physical world, challenging many ideas inherited from classical physics.

As an example, it taught us that each particle can also behave like a wave. Usually the wave associated to an atom has a too short wavelength to be detected. However, when atoms are cooled down to very low temperature, their wave behavior begins to show up since their wavelength is much larger as their velocity is lower: Chapter 6 contains detailed methods used to cool down atoms with lasers, and exploiting the quantum properties of cold atoms. Quantum mechanics is needed to fully understand the electromagnetic field. Understanding some of its properties involves a description in terms of particle flux; this is the field of quantum optics (see Chapter 6). The particles of light are called photons. Unlike atoms, they are massless and they propagate in vacuum with the velocity c.

How can we link photons to electromagnetic waves? A wave is characterized by its frequency, its direction of propagation and its polarization (related to the direction of the electromagnetic field). These parameters define a mode of the quantized electromagnetic field. The spatial and temporal coherence properties of the laser photons come from the fact that they are in a single mode, or in a limited number of modes, of the electromagnetic field.

One may have an idea of the behavior of these photons by comparison with pedestrians (see Figure 1.3): photons emitted by a classical ordinary lamp can be seen as a crowd of people, each of them walking at its own pace in its own direction; at the opposite, in a laser beam, they all march in step like soldiers. These laser photons, *different from others*, are in fact *all the same* and behave collectively!

1.2.   Stimulated Amplification of Radiation

1.2.1.   *Masers and lasers*

The word laser, now commonly used, is the acronym for *Light Amplification by Stimulated Emission of Radiation*. The laser, which was born in 1960, has an elder cousin, named maser (for *Microwave Amplification by Stimulated Emission of Radiation*), born a few years before it, in 1954. Both operate on the same principle, but the maser emits an electromagnetic wave in the microwave range corresponding to centimeter or millimeter wavelengths (masers, especially hydrogen maser, are widely used as frequency standards).

The first lasers were called optical masers. As is clear from their denominations, stimulated emission — also called induced emission — plays a key role in the operation of masers and lasers.

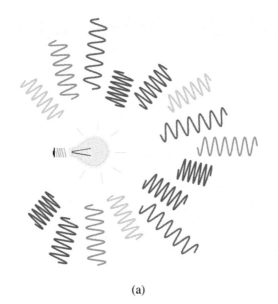

(a)

(b)

Figure 1.3: Photons emitted by a classical lamp (a) have different propagation directions and different wavelengths; photons emitted by a laser (b) all have the same characteristics: direction, frequency, and polarization. In this figure, the oscillations of the electric field, whose spatial period is given by the wavelength, are shown.

1.2.2. *Matter, atoms and energy levels*

Stimulated emission is a light-matter interaction process which may lead to light amplification. At room temperature, matter is composed of atoms, sometimes assembled together to form molecules. In condensed matter (solid or liquid), atoms interact strongly with each other. In the following, we will restrict ourselves to diluted media, such as a gas, to describe atom–light interaction. In a diluted medium, interaction processes are individual: a single atom is involved and a single photon appears or disappears (more than one photon in the case of nonlinear optics, not studied here).

An atom is composed of a positively charged nucleus and of one or more negatively charged electrons. It has been known for almost a century that the binding energy between an electron and the atom, due to interaction

Figure 1.4: Spectrum of the neon atom, emitted by a tube light.

between charges, can only have certain discrete values: the atom energy is quantized.

In 1913, Bohr gave the following description of the interaction between an atom and radiation: the atom can absorb or emit light when it performs a *quantum jump* between two of its energy levels. Let us call E_1 and E_2 the energies of the two involved levels with $E_2 > E_1$. The energy difference satisfies the relation $E_2 - E_1 = h\nu$, where h is the Planck constant, introduced by Planck in 1900 in his study of the blackbody radiation, and ν the radiation frequency. The value of h is 6.6×10^{-34} J.s, which is very small in our international system of units. The product $h\nu$ is the energy of the absorbed or emitted photon so that this relation represents the conservation of energy during the interaction process: in the case of absorption, the energy lost by radiation is given to the atom, and conversely in the case of emission. The lines observed in atomic spectra, as represented in the case of the neon atom in Figure 1.4, originate from energy quantization. As the energy of the atoms can take only discrete values, the same holds true for the frequency — and also the wavelength — of the light they emit or absorb.

1.2.3. Atom–radiation interaction processes

In the following, we assume that the radiation matches the atomic transition. In other words, the radiation frequency obeys the relation $E_2 - E_1 = h\nu$: one talks about optical resonance and the two energy levels involved in the transition are the only ones taken into consideration.

In practice, not only one but a large number of atoms, taken to be all identical, are submitted to the radiation. Some of them are in the energy level E_1, called the ground state and denoted as 1, some others in the energy level E_2, called the excited state and denoted as 2. Physicists call populations the number of atoms per unit volume in each state and denote these populations n_1 and n_2, respectively. In resonant interaction processes between atoms and radiation, the populations are modified as energy is transferred from the atoms to the radiation or conversely.

When Bohr introduced quantum jumps, only two interaction processes were known: absorption and spontaneous emission. During the absorption

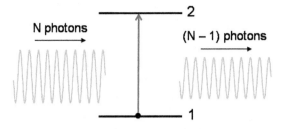

Figure 1.5: During the absorption process, a photon disappears: the intensity of the incident radiation is reduced. The black horizontal lines represent the atomic energy levels. In this example, the energy of level 2 is larger than the energy of level 1.

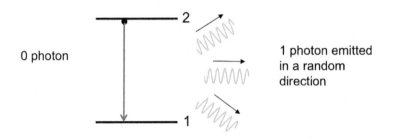

Figure 1.6: During the spontaneous emission process, a photon is created: light is emitted in a random direction.

process, the atom jumps from its ground state to its excited state while absorbing a photon (Figure 1.5); the radiation loses a photon and then its intensity is reduced. During the spontaneous emission process, the atom, initially in its excited state, falls down to its ground state while emitting a photon (Figure 1.6). This photon is randomly emitted in any direction after a certain time spent by the atom in the excited state. This time is random too: its mean value is called the *lifetime* of the excited state. As pointed out by its name, spontaneous emission does not need incident radiation to induce it.

In an article published in 1917, Einstein suggested a third process, induced, or stimulated, emission which is the opposite of absorption and which occurs only in the presence of an incoming radiation, resonant with the transition frequency. During the stimulated emission process, the atom jumps from its excited state to its ground state while emitting a photon (Figure 1.7). This is a coherent phenomenon: if the incoming photons are in

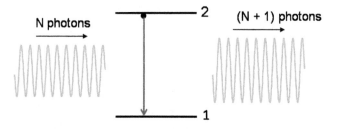

Figure 1.7:   The stimulated emission process induces the appearance of a photon in the same mode of the electromagnetic field as the incident wave: this one is then amplified.

a given mode of the electromagnetic field, the stimulated photon is emitted in the same mode. The incident radiation is then amplified.

1.2.4. *Light amplification*

We just mentioned that if atoms are shone with a resonant light beam, light is amplified due to stimulated emission. But, at the same time, absorption reduces its intensity. These two processes occur simultaneously with spontaneous emission. The question is then: can stimulated emission dominate the other process? Einstein demonstrated that absorption and stimulated emission occur with probabilities given by the same expression, the only difference being that the first one is proportional to the population n_1 of the ground state whereas the second one is proportional to the population n_2 of the excited state. Stimulated emission would then dominate absorption if the condition $n_2 > n_1$ is satisfied: in this case, physicists say that they have performed a population inversion. This condition is not easy to obtain as the atom is usually in its level of lowest energy, its ground state, to which spontaneous emission always takes it back. It is its normal state at thermal equilibrium. To force the atom to leave this ground state, one needs to supply the energy that will bring it to its excited state. This is the pumping process. If the pumping realizes the population inversion, then light can be amplified by atoms.

1.2.5. *The pumping*

Pumping consists of increasing the population of level 2 while decreasing the population of level 1 to obey the condition $n_2 > n_1$ temporarily or permanently. For this purpose, some energy has to be provided to the atoms, a part of which will be given back by the atoms to the photons due to radiation amplification at the frequency ν. Different pumping methods are available, electric, chemical, and optical, depending on the energy source.

Let us focus on the optical pumping method. The energy may come from a classical source with no frequency selection or from a laser. But a pumping beam at frequency ν, resonant with the transition between the levels 1 and 2, cannot achieve population inversion. Indeed, even an intense beam would lead at best to the balance of the populations $n_1 = n_2$ as it would induce stimulated emission and absorption transitions at equivalent rates. Consequently, population inversion cannot be reached with two-level optical pumping: at least three levels are needed.

In the case of three-level pumping mechanism (Figure 1.8(a)), the population of the energy level E_2 is increased due to absorption from the lowest energy level to a higher one, followed by spontaneous emission. The energy

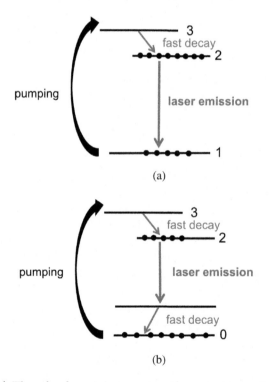

(a)

(b)

Figure 1.8: (a) Three-level pumping process: the pumping mechanism empties level 1 and level 2 is populated by fast decay from a third level; (b) Four-level pumping process: level 1 is not the atomic ground state, and its population can be much smaller than the ground state population.

level E_1 is partially emptied. This kind of pumping system has been developed by Theodor Maiman to carry out the first laser operation in which the amplifying medium consisted of chromium ions embedded in a ruby rod (more details are given in Chapter 2 and especially in Figure 2.6).

In the case of four-level pumping mechanism (Figure 1.8(b)), the energy level E_1 is not the atomic ground state anymore: it is then possible to increase the population of the higher level of the transition of interest while keeping the lower one almost empty as the atom spontaneously decays to the ground state. This pumping system is more efficient than the three-level one, and consequently it is suitable for lasers operating in the continuous regime. This process has been used for the first time to pump helium–neon lasers: the population inversion occurs between two excited levels of atomic neon, the one of higher energy being populated by collisions with helium atoms in the gas discharge. The first helium–neon laser was built by Ali Javan in 1961 (see Chapter 2 and especially Figure 2.1).

1.3.   The Laser Cavity

1.3.1.   *From an amplifier to an oscillator*

We saw in the last section that atom-induced light amplification was possible. This effect may occur in a gaseous, solid, or liquid atomic or molecular medium only if the population inversion between the energy levels corresponding to the resonant transition is achieved. To obtain the laser effect, the next step consists of converting the light amplifier into an oscillator. This transformation is commonly carried out in the field of electronics: to obtain oscillations, the amplifier output is plugged to one of its inputs, in other words, one performs a feedback loop.

Painful to the ears, the Larsen effect is an example of conversion of an amplifier to an oscillator in the electro-acoustic field. The building blocks are a microphone, an amplifier and a loudspeaker. If the loudspeaker faces the microphone, the signal circulating between them is amplified several times by the amplifier. This leads to a shrilly sound whose frequency depends on the characteristics of the amplifier and on the distance between the microphone and the loudspeaker. It is not necessary to speak in the microphone to obtain the Larsen effect. Indeed, the oscillation starts from *noise*, i.e., from the acoustic fluctuations of the environment. A laser operates in the same way: the light, i.e., the electromagnetic wave, oscillation starts from spontaneous emission which acts like a *noise*.

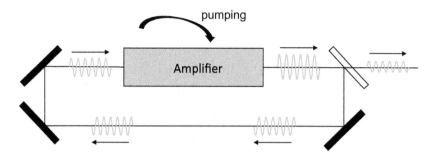

Figure 1.9: Conversion of an optical amplifier into an oscillator (laser): a set of mirrors sends the light at the output of the amplifier back to the input.

To get an optical feedback loop in a laser, the light is sent back to the amplifying medium by a set of mirrors. A phase condition must be fulfilled at each pass of the light wave through the gain medium in order to actually amplify the light circulating in the laser. In other words, the cavity built with mirrors should be a resonant cavity whose length is a multiple of the wavelength of light inside it (see next section). Figure 1.9 is an example of a four-mirror cavity, a ring rectangular cavity, in which light makes *roundtrips*. One of the mirrors, called the output mirror, has a small transmission factor: the light going through it is the output beam of the laser.

To summarize, a laser is a coherent light source consisting of an optical amplifier pumped by an energy source and placed inside a resonant cavity.

1.3.2. *The Fabry–Perot cavity*

The simplest laser cavity is formed by two mirrors facing each other. It is called a Fabry–Perot cavity. This geometry is linear (by comparison with the "ring geometry", in which at least three mirrors are needed) and is widely used for interferometric measurements. In this kind of cavity, one of the mirrors totally reflects the light at a given wavelength whereas the other one transmits a few percents of the intra-cavity light power: the transmitted light provides the laser beam.

The light, successively reflected by the two mirrors, makes roundtrips in the cavity. The optical path corresponding to a roundtrip should be a multiple of the wavelength. This is the resonance condition:

$$2L = p\lambda \quad \text{or} \quad L = p\frac{\lambda}{2}, \tag{1.1}$$

where L is the distance between the two mirrors, λ is the wavelength of light and p is an integer. This is a necessary condition for the waves to be in phase and so to constructively interfere regardless of the number of roundtrips performed in the cavity. Consequently, for a given cavity length L, only the wavelengths for which the relation (1.1) is satisfied will be present in the laser beam.

1.3.3. *The laser cavity modes*

Other fields of physics, such as acoustics, provide the same kind of resonance condition. A plucked string of length L, fixed at both ends, presents resonant vibration modes with an integer number of antinodes distributed on the length L: for these modes, L is a multiple of half the wavelength (see Figure 1.10(a)). As the acoustic wavelength is a fraction of a meter, the integer p is small (its value equals 1 or 2 on the figure). In contrast, the optical wavelength, of the order of a micrometer, leads to large values of p. As an example, for $L = 1\,\mathrm{m}$ and $\lambda = 500\,\mathrm{nm}$, one finds $p = 4{,}000{,}000$. The modes corresponding to the different values of p satisfying the condition (1.1) are called longitudinal modes of the cavity (Figure 1.10(b)). The resulting frequencies are almost equal and many modes oscillate together in the optical cavity. The frequency difference between two adjacent modes is given by $\Delta\nu = \frac{c}{2L}$. As c is about 3×10^8 m/s, the frequency difference is 150 MHz in the example given above. Obviously, as we will see in Section 1.3.5, only the modes amplified by the amplifying medium can oscillate in the cavity.

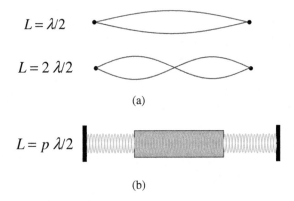

(a)

(b)

Figure 1.10:   (a) Fundamental mode and first harmonic of the resonant modes of a plucked string; (b) Resonant mode of a Fabry–Perot cavity.

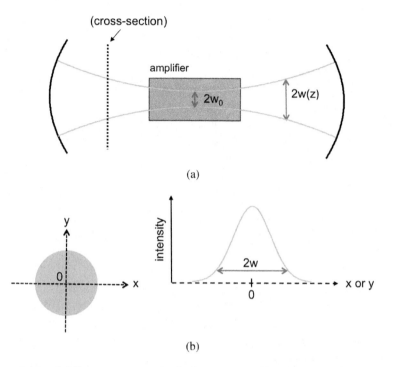

Figure 1.11: (a) Beam geometry in the laser cavity: the transverse dimension of the beam varies. (b) Cross-section and intensity profile of a Gaussian beam.

1.3.4. *The geometry of the beam*

The light wave propagating in the laser cavity is not a plane wave, that is, a wave of infinite transverse extent. At least one of the cavity mirrors should be concave to focus light transversely: all the light is then collected by the mirrors and diffraction losses are limited. The simplest intensity profile is a Gaussian one: in the transverse plane (perpendicular to the propagation direction), the intensity distribution is given by a *bell-shaped curve* of width $2w$. The parameter w is called the *beam radius* (see Figure 1.11(b)). The intensity distribution in the transverse plane obeys the following relation:

$$I(r, z) = I_0(z)e^{-\frac{2r^2}{w^2(z)}}, \tag{1.2}$$

where z is the propagation direction, r is the transverse coordinate, and $I_0(z)$ is the maximum intensity. $2w(z)$ is defined as the width of the curve corresponding to an intensity equals to $I_0(z)/e^2$ which is approximately equal to $0.13\,I_0(z)$. With this geometry, the beam radius varies during the wave propagation in the cavity (Figure 1.11(a)). Its minimal value, w_0, is called *beam waist*. Usually the amplifying medium is located around the beam waist to maximize stimulated emission as the energy density reaches its largest value at this position.

The value of w_0 depends on the radius of curvature of the cavity mirrors. Around the location corresponding to w_0, the light beam diverges slightly. The Rayleigh length is defined as the distance between the beam waist position and the position corresponding to a radius equals to $\sqrt{2}w_0$. During its propagation from the waist position, over a distance equals to the Rayleigh length, the beam transverse size is almost constant, whereas, far from the waist position, the light beam can be seen as a spherical wave: it diverges. The Rayleigh length, z_R, can be written as a function of w_0 and of the wavelength:

$$z_R = \frac{\pi w_0^2}{\lambda}. \tag{1.3}$$

The relation is valid for any kind of laser. For example, in the case of a helium–neon laser ($\lambda = 633\,\text{nm}$), a $600\,\mu\text{m}$ beam waist corresponds to a Rayleigh length of $2\,\text{m}$. It means that over a propagation distance of 2 m, the beam radius remains almost constant. The ability of a laser beam to propagate over large distances with low divergence is the key point for many applications.

However, relation (1.3) tells us that high directivity and small beam waist are not simultaneously achievable. Indeed, the more the beam is focused (using concave mirrors with small curvature radii), the smaller is the w_0, but the larger is the beam divergence (z_R is small too). In practice, the minimum value a light spot diameter can reach is of the order of its wavelength. This is important to store and read a large amount of data on a given area. To this aim, wavelengths as short as possible are chosen: $780\,\text{nm}$ for a CD, $650\,\text{nm}$ for a DVD and $405\,\text{nm}$ for a *Blu-ray Disk* (see also Chapter 3).

1.3.5. *Conditions for laser oscillation*

We previously described the building blocks of a laser. We will now see the requirements to start the laser oscillation. For this purpose, we need to introduce the gain of the amplifier which is proportional to the population difference $n_2 - n_1$: gain is positive if population inversion is achieved.

We have already mentioned that the laser effect starts with spontaneous emission: similar to the Larsen effect, no incident wave is needed. Light

from spontaneous emission is amplified by the atomic or molecular medium
and recycled in the optical cavity for specific wavelengths. To reach the
oscillation regime, the gain of the amplifier should be larger than the losses
for each roundtrip in the cavity. The threshold corresponds to the case
where gain and losses are equal. Below this threshold, the intensity inside
the cavity is negligible. Above the threshold, a laser oscillation is obtained
and a beam is emitted.

Losses are mainly due to mirrors which do not perfectly reflect light.
Obviously, it is the case for the output mirror which should let the laser
beam leave the cavity. Other kinds of losses may exist too: due to the
mirrors (absorption or scattering) or other optical components of the cavity
including the amplifying medium (reflection at the interfaces, diffraction).
These losses should be reduced as much as possible.

In the case of low gain amplifiers, cavity losses have to be very low so
that the gain can overcome them. For most gaseous amplifying media (for
a helium–neon laser, the gain is of the order of 2%), the cavity mirrors
must have high reflection coefficients to allow the laser effect (typically on
the order of 99% for the output mirror). Conversely, laser diodes, made
of semiconductor components, exhibit a high gain: the cavity mirrors are
obtained by cleaving the ends of the material and their reflection coefficient
is due to the difference of optical index between the material and air: it
is of the order of 30%. In this case, the laser effect occurs even with low
reflection mirrors.

The above oscillation condition depends on the wavelength. It is the
case for the gain of the amplifying medium. Indeed, the medium response
is given by a gain curve as presented in Figure 1.12. It is also the case for the
reflection coefficients of the mirrors. And we mentioned in Section 1.3.2 that
the cavity resonance condition is satisfied only for wavelengths associated
with the cavity longitudinal modes. Several modes may obey the condition
that *gain be larger than losses* simultaneously, each of them for its own
wavelength. In this case, the laser operates in a multimode regime: several
adjacent frequencies distant of $c/2L$ are emitted. On the other hand, if
only one mode obeys the condition, the laser operates on a single mode
and a single frequency is emitted. These two kinds of regimes are shown in
Figure 1.12.

Some applications require a single-mode laser. To switch from multimode to single-mode configurations, one can reduce the cavity length
to increase the frequency spacing between adjacent modes or increase the
losses. The best solution consists of filtering a single mode by embedding a

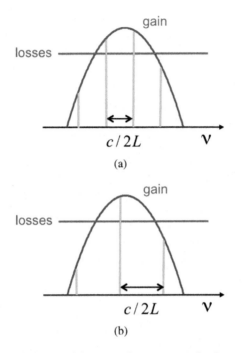

(a)

(b)

Figure 1.12:   Gain of the amplifying medium versus the frequency (blue curve) and cavity modes (green lines), the losses (in red) being constant. (a) If the condition *gain larger than losses* is satisfied for several cavity modes, the laser operates in the multimode regime. (b) If this condition is satisfied only for one mode, the laser operates in the single-mode regime.

frequency selective optical component within the laser cavity. For example, a shorter *intra-cavity* Fabry–Perot can be introduced inside the laser cavity, such as a simple plate of glass with parallel faces. These aspects will be discussed in Chapter 5.

A last comment before the end of this section: we mentioned that the gain corresponding to a mode oscillating in the cavity has to be larger than the losses. Does it mean that the light intensity in the cavity — and then the intensity emitted through the output mirror — will increase indefinitely? In fact, the intensity will reach a limit value, as when the intensity increases, saturation effects cause a reduction of the gain. This is shown in Figure 1.13. For the laser to start, the gain must be larger than the losses, but in the steady-state regime, the laser operates at an intensity for which gain equals losses.

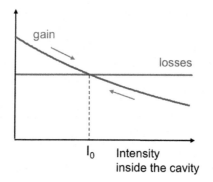

Figure 1.13: Gain of the amplifying medium for a given mode as a function of the cavity intensity (blue curve), the losses (in red) being constant. The operating point, given by the crossing of the two curves, corresponds to an intensity I_0: if the intensity is smaller than I_0, the gain is larger than the losses and the intensity increases; if the intensity is larger than I_0, the gain is smaller than the losses and the intensity decreases.

1.4. The Laser: One Mode of Operation, but Various Realizations

1.4.1. *How a laser operates*

Let us recall again the elements which constitute a laser:

- an amplifier medium, pumped to a state from which it can radiate through stimulated emission of light in a frequency range which is characteristic of the medium,
- an optical cavity which performs the feedback loop: the mirrors send back light in the amplifier medium and define the spatial and temporal (frequency) properties.

The energy of light inside the cavity escapes partly through the output mirror and gives rise to the laser beam.

1.4.2. *An energy converter*

In a laser, the pumping energy provided as electrical, chemical or light energy, is converted into coherent light energy; this energy is concentrated into one or several given modes of resonant radiation inside the optical cavity. The laser yield is defined as the ratio between the light power emitted by the laser and the pumping power. Depending on the kind of laser, this yield varies from one per thousand to 50% (the latter value is obtained in semiconductor lasers).

Classical lamps also have various yields: this yield is only 5% in light bulbs (the energy difference is converted into heat) but it is larger in fluorescent tube lights. The main difference between lamps and lasers is that laser light is emitted in a given direction, and can then be concentrated onto a small surface leading to a very high local illumination. At a distance of one meter, a 100 W light bulb (that means 5 W of light power) delivers an illumination of $0.04\,\text{mW/cm}^2$, while a 5 W laser focused on a $1\,\text{mm}^2$ spot gives rise to a local illumination 10 million times more intense, larger than $500\,\text{W/cm}^2$. This is why laser beams are dangerous for the human eye, the damage threshold of which is about $2\,\text{mW/mm}^2$, that is $0.2\,\text{W/cm}^2$, around the 600 nm wavelength.

1.4.3.   *A large variety of realizations*

Since the first laser that operated in 1960, many different laser devices have been developed. They use amplifying media, either gaseous or liquid or solid (crystals, glasses, and semiconductors), and various pumping methods: optical pumping (with a laser or a flash lamp), electrical pumping, collisional or chemical pumping. Moreover, there is a multiplicity of cavity geometries and mirrors numbers: various linear or ring cavities with three, four or six mirrors. Finally, they can operate in a continuous-wave mode or in a pulsed mode (relaxed, triggered or mode-blocked). We know now how to produce femtosecond pulses ($1\,\text{fs} = 10^{-15}\,\text{s}$), having pulse duration of the order of one light oscillation period (see Chapter 4).

1.4.4.   *Fifty years later, lasers are everywhere*

Due to their remarkable properties, laser beams are used in a lot of applications. From bar codes to laser printers, from storage to reading and transportation of information (see Chapter 3), lasers have transformed our daily life. In construction or in industry, they are universal tools for alignment, drilling, cutting and welding. They enable us to measure contaminating traces (see Chapter 3), distances and velocities. In medicine, they are used as selective and precise tools for therapy (see Chapter 7). Many advances in fundamental research already derive from lasers (see Chapters 6 and 7) and lasers will be widely present in the future to probe matter, control nuclear fusion, detect gravitational waves (see Chapter 5), and surely for many other applications that we do not yet foresee.

Chapter 2

Lasers of All Sizes

Philippe Balcou

CNRS Senior Researcher,
Centre Lasers Intenses et Applications,
Université de Bordeaux, Talence, France

Sébastien Forget

Associate Professor, Université Paris 13,
Laboratoire de Physique des Lasers, Villetaneuse, France

Isabelle Robert-Philip

CNRS Researcher,
Laboratoire de Photonique et de Nanostructures,
Marcoussis, France

2.1. Introduction

Lasers produce a controlled, pure and concentrated light, which differs from the light emitted by conventional sources, such as the sun, incandescent bulbs or fluorescent tubes. The "light concentration" offered by lasers makes them attractive for many applications: lasers can cut, weld or measure the earth surface from a satellite. Laser light can also help curing locally injured areas (see Chapter 7), carry messages over the internet (see Chapter 3), etc.

For each of these applications, a specific type of laser is used: indeed, if all of them operate on the same principle (stimulated emission coupled with an optical cavity, as explained in Chapter 1), each of them is very different from the others. Lasers can be of various sizes and power, use all kinds of materials (liquid, solid or gaseous) and can emit almost every color (from X-rays to far infrared, including of course all the colors of the visible spectrum). They may emit continuously (CW for "Continuous Wave" operation) or in the form of flashes, always shorter and more powerful. In this chapter, we invite you to a short journey through all types of lasers: have a nice trip!

2.2.　The Laser in All Its Forms

Let us begin with a reminder of the principles outlined in Chapter 1: To get laser light, you need to place an amplifying medium inside an optical cavity, which is a sort of cage that traps light. This amplifying medium constitutes the core of the device. It is customary to classify lasers according to the nature of their amplifying medium: gas, liquid or solid. In this section, we will review all these types of lasers following this classification.

2.2.1.　*Gas lasers*

As suggested by its name, the amplifying medium in a gas laser consists of a gas or a gas mixture, usually contained in a glass or quartz tube. This gas emits light when excited by an electrical discharge. This is the same principle used in the fluorescent tubes that produce white or colored light for lighting or luminous signs. To build a laser, the tube enclosing the gas mixture is placed in an optical cavity usually formed by two facing mirrors. This cavity can amplify light, select the emitted color and concentrate the light beam in a given direction. Among the various gases used for lasing, the most common are argon, mixtures of helium and neon, carbon dioxide mixed with nitrogen and helium or the so-called "excimers" containing a mixture of rare gas and halogen (such as xenon and chlorine or krypton and fluorine).

Of course, the gas cannot create light out of nothing. It can only transmit and amplify light if energy is available: this energy supply is called excitation or more often "pumping". In gas lasers, pumping is usually provided by an electrical power source: it is very convenient since the only thing you have to do to make the laser work is to plug it into the wall! Everything begins with the collision of electrons (from the discharge or electric current) with atoms or molecules of the gas. These atoms or molecules can then be ionized (they gain or lose an electron) then excited to a higher energy level, and finally emit and amplify light. This is the operating principle of argon or krypton lasers. Sometimes the process is a bit more complicated and you need another "go-between" gas: for example,

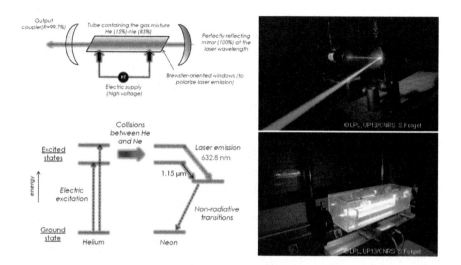

Figure 2.1: Principle of the helium–neon laser. In the diagram (top left), we recognize the tube which encloses the gas mixture. This tube is inserted into a cavity that traps light and lets only a small fraction escape from one side (left here). The energy source allowing the gas mixture to emit and amplify light is electricity. It will give its energy to helium atoms, which, in turn, will transfer this energy to neon atoms through collisions. The now excited neon atoms will then emit red light. Two pictures of helium–neon lasers show the straight red beam emitted by the laser. We also see, isolated in a transparent box, the tube which contains the radiant gas mixture. The length of the cavity is usually of a few tens of centimeters.

in the well-known helium–neon laser whose principle is shown in Figure 2.1, helium does not emit light. It is excited to a high-energy level by the electric current and then simply transmits this energy to the neon atoms through collisions between the two types of atoms. It is the latter which will then go back to a lower energy level, releasing the corresponding energy in the form of red photons characteristic of neon. Another example is the carbon dioxide laser (also called CO_2 Laser): the carbon dioxide molecules, which will finally provide infrared light, are excited by collisions with nitrogen molecules, themselves being excited by an electrical discharge. Finally, for excimer lasers, the species that produce light are obtained by chemical reaction between halogen (e.g., fluorine) and inert gas molecules (argon, krypton, xenon, etc.), excited by the electric current. In the atoms which produce light, the electrons can occupy only certain well-defined energy levels. Indeed, one atom consists of a nucleus concentrating substantially all of its mass, and the electrons are distributed around the nucleus to form an extensive cloud. The electron distribution is not uniform in space: there are areas where the chance of finding them is greater. We call these regions "orbitals". Each orbital can be occupied by only two electrons, and is characterized by an extremely well-defined energy. The color of the light produced by the laser depends only on the energy level of the atoms constituting the amplifying medium: consequently, each gas generates a specific color or set of colors. You can remember some of them: argon lasers emit in the violet and blue-green (especially 488 and 514 nm), the majority of helium–neon lasers produce red light (633 nm) and excimer lasers emit in the ultraviolet (e.g., 193 nm for the argon/fluorine mixture). As for carbon dioxide lasers, they emit in the mid-infrared, around 10 microns, so no chance to see their light beam with the naked eye!

The beam of light produced by gas lasers is of exceptional quality. It is highly concentrated in space (we say it is very directional), and its color, very pure, is concentrated around a single wavelength (in other words, these lasers emit very narrow spectral lines). Finally, the luminous power radiated by these lasers ranges from a few milliwatts (for helium–neon lasers) to a few tens of watts (for argon lasers), and even nearly 100 kilowatts with carbon dioxide lasers.

However, gas lasers are very inefficient: a large number of electrons is required to supply a single photon in the laser beam. When the power is important (from a few watts), a large part of the electrical energy is lost as heat during the excitation process. Therefore, the laser has to be cooled, for example by circulating water around the tube. Generally speaking, gas lasers are often bulky lasers, with optical cavities ranging from a few tens of centimeters (for helium–neon lasers, for example) to a few meters (for high power argon lasers).

2.2.2. *Dye lasers*

In dye lasers, the amplifying medium is liquid. It is composed of a solution enclosed in a glass cell, which contains organic dye molecules. Such a solution is obtained from a powder of dye molecules, dissolved in solvents (in general alcoholic ones). A typical example is rhodamine 6G, a bronze-colored powder which, after dissolution in alcohol, emits light in the orange-red part of the spectrum under green light illumination.

How is a dye laser (such as the one depicted in Figure 2.2) built? Simply place the glass bowl containing the dye in an optical cavity formed by two

Figure 2.2: Picture of a liquid dye laser excited by an argon laser. The blue-green beam is the beam of the gas laser which delivers the excitation light. We see from the top of the picture, the pipe for circulating the red dye solution from a reservoir. These dyes excited by the argon laser emit a yellow-orange beam that can be seen in the picture (Copyright CNRS Photothèque/Serge Equilbey, Laboratoire Charles Fabry, Institut d'Optique Graduate School).

mirrors. Pumping is however a whole different ball game: the dye molecules in dilute alcohol are not able to properly conduct electric current, and therefore one cannot use electricity to excite molecules, unlike gas lasers. The energy required to excite the gain medium must be supplied with light. This light can be emitted by another laser (such as a gas laser or a solid-state laser) or by an arc lamp that delivers intense flashes.

Dye lasers emit mostly visible light, so that we can then see the laser beam with the naked eye (see Figure 2.2). The main advantage of this type of lasers, which has made them very popular for years, is the fact that you can easily change the color of the emitted laser beam. Firstly, there is a tremendous amount of dye molecules, each of them able to emit in a given range of colors: simply select the right molecule for the desired color. But most interesting is that each molecule can indeed produce several wavelengths: this is because, unlike atoms used in gas lasers which have only a few energy levels with well-defined energies, complex molecules in a liquid dye have a huge number of energy levels very close to each other; the lasing effect can occur between any of these levels, so that different energies — and then colors — may be emitted. It is said that these lasers are widely tunable and it is an exceptional feature for lasers. How do you choose the exact color of the laser beam? This is done using either narrow spectral filters inserted into the resonator (see Chapter 5), or specific mirrors (called diffraction gratings) to close the cavity: the color of the light reflected by those mirrors is slightly changed by rotating the mirror around its axis. Thus, rhodamine 6G lasers can radiate laser light from the yellow (at a wavelength near 570 nm) to the red (at a wavelength of 640 nm); the color emitted by stilbene lasers can extend from the violet (390 nm) to the blue (430 nm), etc.

Being able to change the color of the laser radiation on demand is a considerable advantage. In addition, we will see later that having a wide spectrum (several colors available) is a prerequisite to produce ultrashort flashes of light: it is from dye lasers that the first ultrashort pulses of laser light were born, with duration around one hundred of femtoseconds, or several thousands of billion times shorter than a second!

However, despite all their qualities, dye lasers are nowadays less and less used. Why? Well, simply because their implementation is very difficult. The dye solution degrades over time and must be changed regularly. Moreover, it is often composed of solvents (methanol, etc.) that are bad for your health. Equally annoying: the molecules are destroyed by light excitation, so that the laser can only operate continuously if a permanent dye circulation is enabled between the glass bowl and a reservoir, through a system of pipes. This requires hydraulic pumps and makes the system operation cumbersome. Finally, the dye must be most often excited by other relatively powerful lasers, which are themselves very massive. An interesting alternative is the recent development of organic solid-state dye laser, where dye molecules are embedded in a solid matrix. These devices then mimic solid-state lasers (see next section) while keeping some of the most interesting capabilities of dye molecules such as wide tunability.

2.2.3. *Solid-state lasers*

The amplifying medium can also be a solid. This solid can be a piece of crystal or glass, an optical fiber or very specific materials called semiconductors. Inserted in an optical cavity, those solids can become lasers, called solid-state lasers, fiber lasers and laser diodes respectively.

In a large majority of solid-state lasers, crystals are used as amplifying medium. These crystals are nothing else but the precious or semi-precious gems used in jewelry: ruby, sapphire, garnet, etc. Crystals in lasers are generally shaped as rods or parallelepipeds of millimeter dimensions. In this case, the optical cavity is formed around the crystal, either by coating two opposite surfaces of the crystal with a reflective material, or by placing the crystal between two mirrors. However, it is not the glass or crystal itself that radiates light, but rather the metal ions that are artificially included in the crystalline or glassy matrix. Those metal ions are derived from either the so-called transition metals (chromium or titanium for example), or rare earths (such as neodymium or ytterbium), which contrary to what their name suggests, are pretty common. It is with this type of gain medium that lasing was obtained for the first time in 1960. The crystal was then ruby, which is alumina crystal containing chromium ions that give the famous red color (and the laser effect). Since then, other crystals and glasses as well as other ions were used. Among the most commonly used today, we can quote yttrium and aluminium garnet (or YAG) containing ions which emit in the infrared (neodymium, at a wavelength of 1064 nm, or ytterbium around 1030 nm).

The color of the radiated laser beam changes not only with the ion used, but also slightly with the crystal that contains it. Thus, if we replace yttrium and aluminium garnet by glass, the color radiated by the neodymium ion is slightly shifted to the visible spectrum: the wavelength emission drops from 1064 to 1053 nm.

A particular case deserves special consideration: by inserting titanium ions in a matrix of sapphire, we obtain a laser capable of radiating light from the red (around 700 nm) to the infrared (around 1000 nm), just like dye lasers but with a range of colors even larger. These are titanium–sapphire lasers (see Figure 2.3), which are now used to create ultrashort and ultra-intense flashes of light: we shall explore this later.

When glass is used, it can also be shaped in the form of a parallelepiped or rod, but it is more interesting to stretch it to form a fiber thinner than a hair: the famous and widely used optical fiber that carries our telephone communications and all the information exchanged on the Internet (see Chapter 3). By inserting ions — usually rare earth elements (ytterbium, erbium or thulium) — in the fiber and placing mirrors at both ends, we obtain a laser fiber: this type of laser (see Figure 2.4) allows a very efficient heat dissipation over the entire length of the fiber, and they can consequently generate extremely powerful beams. Optical fibers are also used not as a laser medium themselves, but coupled to other lasers: for telecommunications, for example (see Chapter 3) or to generate wavelengths different from that of the initial laser (these are non-linear effects — shown in Figure 2.4).

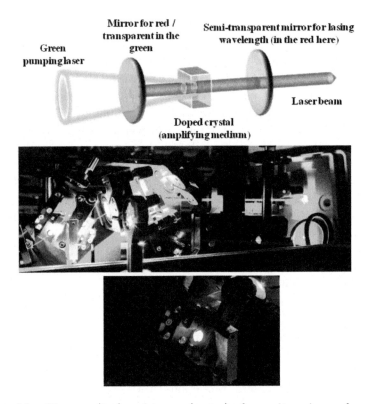

Figure 2.3: Diagram (top) and image (center) of a cavity using as laser gain medium a sapphire matrix doped with titanium ions. A green beam, from an argon laser or a frequency-doubled neodymium laser provides the optical energy necessary to excite the titanium ions. The very bright point on the left side is the position of the sapphire crystal. Titanium ions then radiate red light. The photograph below is a magnified view of the crystal.

Solid-state lasers are very popular: they are stable, compact and provide high quality beams together with high optical powers. They are able to produce continuous light, but also short or ultrashort pulses. To allow laser light emission in solid-state lasers or fibers, the excitation energy is here again provided by the light from another laser or from intense flashes. Again, we cannot directly excite the ions by electric current. Semiconductor lasers (or laser diodes) are very often used for excitation, as they can themselves use an electrical excitation.

But what exactly is a diode laser? It is a laser using another kind of artificial solid-state material, called semiconductors, as gain medium.

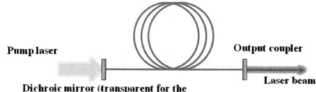

Pump laser

Output coupler

Laser beam

Dichroic mirror (transparent for the
pump, highly reflective for the laser)

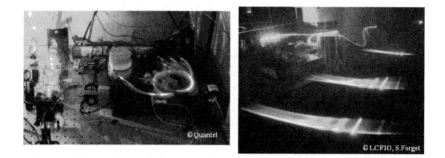

© Quantel

© LCFIO, S.Forget

Figure 2.4: Principle of a fiber laser. Silica doped with rare earth ions is stretched to form a thin fiber of a few meters, tens or hundreds of meters long. At both ends of the fiber, high-reflection mirrors are positioned. The rare earth ions are excited by another laser source (shown here in green). The laser produces a beam of infrared light. Bottom left: Image of a fiber laser (Quantel). Bottom right: Nonlinear effects (Raman here) in a fiber: a green laser is sent through an optical fiber (in the background) and new wavelengths are generated (made visible by dispersion on a diffraction grating).

A semiconductor is a crystal with very specific properties: it carries electrical current less efficiently than metals (such as copper wires that bring electricity to our homes) but better than insulators (such as air, glass or plastics such as PVC). To understand how such a material can emit light, consider first an isolated atom. The atom has distinct energy levels for electrons. A crystal is formed when a large number of atoms are placed close to each other in a regular geometric arrangement. Therefore, the electron distribution changes: the electron energies are not well-defined anymore (as for isolated atoms) but are distributed over intervals called energy bands. When the temperature is close to the lowest in the universe ($-273.15°C$ or $0\,K$), the electrons are concentrated in the lower energy bands. The difference between semiconductors and other crystals is that for semiconductors, the energy difference between the highest energy band completely filled with electrons and the energy band just above (in energy), which is almost empty of electrons, is small.

How can we generate light from a semiconductor? Whereas the energy radiated by an atom comes from the energy released when an electron falls from one atomic orbital to another, the energy radiated from a semiconductor is provided when an electron transits from one band to another one of lower energy. However, not all semiconductor materials can produce light. Some of them, such as silicon or germanium, though widely used in microelectronics, are useless as laser media. Much more interesting are gallium arsenide or indium phosphide, which have the strong advantage of being luminescent. The light is mainly emitted in the red and extends into the infrared part of the spectrum, depending on the material chosen. To provide the energy needed to promote the electrons toward the highest energy band, a source of electric current is generally used. This is the principle of light emitting diodes or LEDs, which can be found on the cars dashboards, on calculators, in bicycles' backlights, on remote controls, etc. To make a laser, it is often not necessary to use additional mirrors to form the optical cavity: we simply use the opposite sides of the semiconductor crystal, because the interface between the crystal and the air is an acceptable mirror by itself (see top of Figure 2.5). You can also choose to integrate mirrors close to the amplifier medium. This is the case of vertical cavity lasers as shown in Figure 2.5.

Laser diodes are interesting because of their low cost and high efficiency: semiconductor lasers are now of utmost importance and account for a large part of the total economic market for lasers. They are used to carry information exchanged by phone or internet (Section 3.1), they read DVDs (Section 3.2) or bar codes in supermarkets, etc. It is also thanks to laser diodes that everyone can own a laser: they are the core of small red laser pointers sold everywhere for a few euros. Why did these lasers become so important? One reason is their low manufacturing cost, with the ability to make thousands of items at the same time. Another point is their excellent efficiency and compactness (see Figures 2.5 and 3.2): they are only a few tenths of a millimeter large and only some microns thick (about 20 times less than the thickness of an aluminium sheet). However, the laser light they produce is generally less directional (because the size of the cavity is very small) and not as spectrally "pure" as other lasers (especially gas lasers).

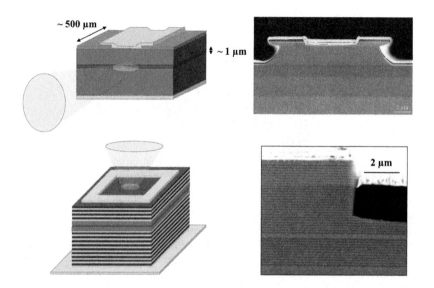

Figure 2.5: Top left, schematic diagram of a ribbon semiconductor laser. In red at the center, we see the material that emits light. The top and bottom metal layers provide the current needed to excite the material. Finally, the laser cavity is simply obtained by using the opposite sides of the semiconductor as mirrors. A picture taken with an electron microscope (upper right) shows one of these two faces (Copyright CNRS Photo Library/Pierre Grech, Didier Cot, Yves Rouillard, Aurore Vicet; South Institute of Electronics (IES), Montpellier, France). In yellow, you can see the metal electrical contact and in red the area that produces infrared light. Below, we present a new architecture of semiconductor laser, radiating laser light not from the side but vertically. The amplifying medium, in red, is surrounded by two semiconductor mirrors made of a stack of different layers of semiconductor materials. The yellow metal layers are used to bring the electrical current needed to excite the amplifying medium. An electron microscope picture shows (bottom right) a cross-section of such a laser (Copyright CNRS Laboratory for Photonics and Nanostructures, Marcoussis, France).

2.3. Lasers for Every Taste

2.3.1. *The rise of lasers*

Stimulated emission, at the heart of laser oscillation, is a natural phenomenon but arises in nature solely under extreme conditions which are neither present nor achievable on Earth. For instance, in the 1970's, precise astronomical observations revealed that laser amplifiers existed (without

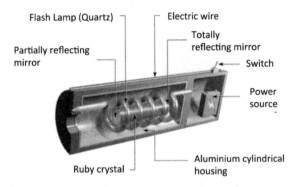

Figure 2.6: Schematics of the first laser realized by Theodore Maiman. The basic element is a cylinder made of ruby. Chromium ions in the ruby are optically excited by a lamp delivering very intense flashes of white light. This electrically-powered lamp is a tube containing Xenon gas under high pressure; this tube is rolled around the cylinder. The laser cavity is built by coating the facets of the ruby cylinder with reflecting metallic layers.

any mirrors!) in the Universe, in particular, in sufficiently dense interstellar clouds excited by light radiated from stars.

In order to harness stimulated emission and build a laser on Earth, one had in a first place to discover on paper such an effect, first introduced by Albert Einstein in 1917. The first laser was however built many years later in 1960 by Theodore Maiman (see Figure 2.6 as well as the preface by Charles Townes), thanks to the pioneering theoretical work of Charles Townes and Arthur Schawlow. In his experiment, Theodore Maiman, an American physicist, had noticed that chromium atoms inside a ruby crystal radiated red light when they were shone by intense bursts of flashlights. In order to produce laser light, one ingredient was however still lacking: an optical cavity, that he built by simply coating each facets of the ruby crystal cylinder with reflective aluminium layers. The first beam of directive, intense and monochromatic coherent light was thus produced.

This first laser resulted from a long period of very intensive work in fundamental science, with the introduction of the concept and theory of stimulated light emission by Albert Einstein in 1917, the amplification of microwaves by stimulated emission by Charles Townes in 1953, the physics of optical excitation by Alfred Kastler. Nobody had foreseen at that time the numerous applications of such light sources in a wide variety of fields; at best one envisioned that they could help to further improve our understanding in the rather specialized research field of molecular spectroscopy.

Lasers however left out of the laboratory at the speed of light (or nearly. . .) and rapidly found practical applications: they have been treating diseases (in particular, in ophthalmology) since the beginning of the 1960's, drilling since 1965, cutting since 1967, reading bar codes since 1974. . .

If laser light is involved nowadays in a large number of applications, lasers did not desert laboratories. They are still a research topic, that aims at reducing their size, making them cheaper, shortening the flashes of light they radiate, increasing the power they deliver or producing laser light in color ranges still difficult to reach, such as far infrared or X rays.

2.3.2. *Lasers of all sizes*

Physicists always aim at coming up with new ideas and pushing the boundaries and limits of knowledge. Laser physicists are not exceptions to this rule. For instance, lasers start at present to enter the nanoworld: The smallest laser to date is 5000 times smaller than the stroke of a pen (see Figure 2.7). It consists of a very thin rod of semiconductor embedding the gain material; the laser cavity is built by coating the rod with metal. At this level of miniaturization, the operation of such lasers cannot be fully understood by use of traditional classical laser theories and requires new modeling tools from the field of quantum physics.

On the opposite side, some lasers can display dimensions exceeding 100 meters. One example is the Laser Mégajoule (see Figure 2.8), near Bordeaux in France, which concentrates 176 laser beams in a 300 meter-building, capable to accommodate an aircraft carrier. This exceptional laser will gradually reach full power between 2014 and 2018. The construction site is impressive: a 40,000 m² building, 125 tons of glass optical amplifier and 9,000 m² of optical interfaces!

2.3.3. *The colors of the rainbow. . . and beyond*

In contrast with other conventional light sources (sun, incandescent lamps etc.), lasers deliver a concentrate of light, spatially (the famous directive laser beam) as well as spectrally. While the light emitted by the sun contains all visible colors and even invisible wavelengths (like infrared and ultraviolet light), laser light is most of the time concentrated at a single color: it is referred to as "monochromatic" light.

As explained in Chapter 1, the color of the light emitted by a laser is determined by the choice of the amplifying medium. Depending on the chosen gaseous, solid or liquid gain material, the laser light will be blue, red

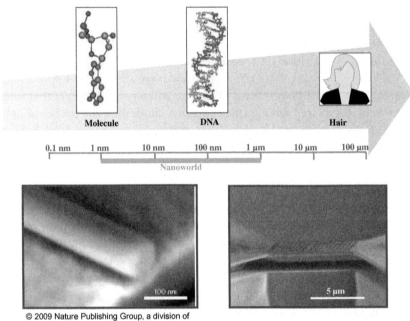

Figure 2.7:   Lasers are presently getting smaller and smaller, as small as a DNA strand, 100 times bigger than a molecule and 1,000 thinner than a hair. The figure on the bottom left shows one example (Credit Prof. Xiang Zhang, UC Berkeley; Copyright (2009) Nature Publishing Group). This laser is one of the smallest lasers in the world. It consists of a cylinder made of semiconductor which acts as the material gain; the cavity is built by coating the cylinder with metal. Another strategy used to reduce the dimensions of the lasers is shown on the right: the laser cavity is built by suspending a thin layer of semiconductor (100 thinner than an aluminium foil), adequately pierced by an array of holes to form a mirror (Copyright CNRS-Laboratoire de Photonique et de Nanostructures, Marcoussis, France). Again, the gain material is made of semiconductor. Such a laser is not much bigger than a red blood cell.

or invisible to the naked eye, in the infrared or ultraviolet (see Figure 2.9). To produce laser light in the ultraviolet, one uses argon or excimer lasers; argon lasers are also used to produce blue and red light, the latter being also emitted by gas lasers (helium–neon or krypton) and solid-state lasers (semiconductor or ruby). To reach the infrared, the gain material usually consists of semiconductors or yttrium–aluminium garnet doped with neodymium ions. In the mid-infrared, one uses carbon dioxide laser as well as unconventional semiconductor lasers named quantum cascade lasers.

Figure 2.8: On the left is shown the building hosting the Laser MégaJoule (LMJ), the second largest laser in the world, near Bordeaux in France. This laser plays a major role in the investigation of matter under extreme conditions, with potential applications in energy production by inertial fusion, as well as laboratory astrophysical experiments (Copyright Didier Fosse/G2I Vertigo). On the right is shown the 10 meter-large interaction chamber of the LMJ, in which 160 compression laser beams and 16 diagnostic laser beams are concentrated on a microsphere with a sub-millimeter diameter and containing cooled deuterium and tritium. Various configurations will be studied : direct focusing of the laser beams on the sphere, focusing in an auxiliary cylinder, use of a Petawatt laser to trigger the fusion reactions (Copyright CEA).

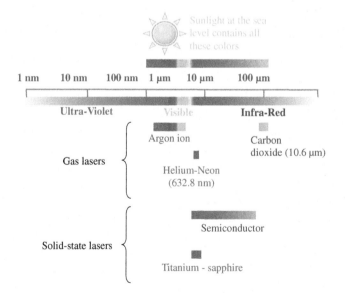

Figure 2.9: The color of the laser light will depend on the material forming the optical amplifier. Much of the spectrum can be covered, from the ultraviolet to the infrared.

Most lasers produce single-color light. However, some of them can deliver light over a certain spectral range. For instance, the color of the light radiated by the titanium–sapphire laser can be tuned from the red to the infrared. This is also the case of dye lasers or some semiconductor lasers. The emitted color is hereafter selected by precise optical adjustments, based on the use of filters that transmit only one single color, or the use of diffraction gratings or mirrors that reflect differently each color depending on their orientation.

2.3.4. *Shorter and shorter lasers*

In addition to their ability to emit light which is concentrated in terms of color spectrum, lasers can also be concentrated in time. While they can indeed operate in a continuous way, they are also able to supply very short flashes of light, called "laser pulses". Thanks to a continuous flow of new ideas and technological improvements, laser physicists keep on demonstrating shorter and shorter flashes, up to the point where these pulses only last today few femtoseconds, namely, one million billion times shorter than a second. To draw a parallel, the ratio between a femtosecond and a second, is the same as that between the width of a human hair, and the distance between Earth and Sun! How possibly can such short light pulses be produced? Basically two methods are to be used: one is called mode-locking, and the other Q-switching.

Let us start with the mode-locking method, with one specific implementation illustrated in Figure 2.10 (other mode-locking techniques are described in Chapter 4). If one considers very pure laser light, made of one single color, the wave aspect of light is not compatible with very short pulse durations, which cannot be of the order or smaller than one period of oscillation of the electromagnetic field. Indeed, a few light cycles are necessary for its color to be well defined. This is a very general property of waves, which for light establishes a link between the color and the pulse duration: if the laser light is concentrated over a tiny interval of colors within the rainbow, and therefore is known with high accuracy, then the timing of the pulse will be largely spread over time. Quite straightforwardly, this principle tells us that it is not possible to generate a very short pulse, while keeping the light spectrum concentrated in the close vicinity of one single color. This does contrast with our previous assessment about lasers being well concentrated in the color spectrum, meaning having a very well-defined wavelength. Then how could very short light flashes be generated in such

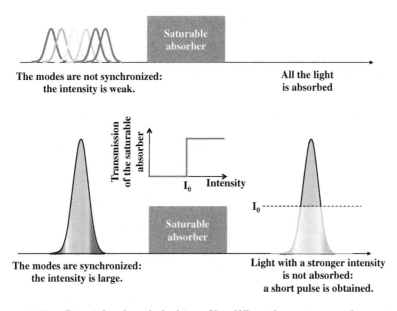

The modes are not synchronized: the intensity is weak.

All the light is absorbed

The modes are synchronized: the intensity is large.

Light with a stronger intensity is not absorbed: a short pulse is obtained.

Figure 2.10: Principle of mode-locking. Up: When the various modes, or individual colors, are not synchronized, they are blocked by the saturable absorber. In contrast, when they are emitted at the same time, and hence are synchronized (bottom), then the resulting light intensity is greatly enhanced, and gets sufficient to peek through the saturable absorber: an ultrashort laser pulse is then transmitted.

conditions? We have no choice: we must generate light over a full interval of wavelengths, and not just one single color. For instance, a 10 femtosecond pulse (1 femtosecond $= 10^{-15}$ s) extends over a very large range of colors, with a width around 100 nanometers in the light spectrum. To give an idea of how large this is, we may note that such a width, assumed to lie in the middle of the visible colors, would correspond to one-third of the range of all colors detected by the eye, from green to yellow, then orange, and up to red. This leads directly to one technological constraint: only amplifying media able to emit light over a similar broad range of colors can be used, e.g., dye molecules, or sapphire doped with titanium ions. However, this is not sufficient yet: we need all those colors to combine in phase so as to generate short pulses, as will be detailed in Chapter 4 (especially Figure 4.1).

To synchronize all these colors, one may add an additional element in the laser cavity, called a saturable absorber. This is a very special material, whose working principle is presented in Figure 2.10. It is designed to remain opaque as long as the light power remains weak, but then to bleach and become transparent for intense light. This element creates a positive transmission bias for really short pulses, so that, within a laser cavity, only very short — and hence intense — laser pulses are not absorbed, but can oscillate in the cavity. The resulting duration of short pulses is inversely proportional to the spectral linewidth available for emission, that depends on the physical and chemical characteristics of the active medium. A titanium-doped sapphire crystal has a broad emission bandwidth, and can support pulses of few femtoseconds only!

Let us now describe the other approach, the Q-switch regime (Figure 2.11). Understanding this process requires to recall briefly about the general mechanism of lasers, already mentioned in Chapter 1. The key element is an amplifying medium, which incorporates atoms, molecules, ions etc., which are excited by feeding them with energy from an external source — whether through an electrical current, or an auxiliary light source. When a suitable light wave illuminates the excited active medium, then the atoms, ions, molecules etc. will release part of this energy, and transfer it to the incoming laser — a process called stimulated emission. As mentioned in Chapter 1, this is however not sufficient to induce the

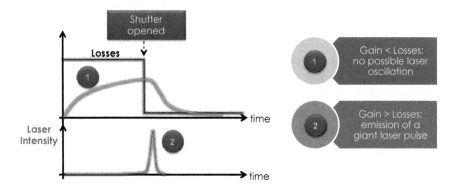

Figure 2.11: Principle of generation of laser light flashes in a Q-switch regime. In a first step, a shutter located within the cavity is kept dark, thus preventing the light wave to go through the amplifier, and hindering amplification. No laser light will be produced. The amplifying medium remains however subject to external irradiation or excitation, bringing more and more atoms or molecules to excited levels, and storing energy gradually. The shutter is then suddenly opened, switching the losses to low values. Immediately, light pulses can perform roundtrips past the amplifier, and reach increasingly high intensities. Most of the energy stored in the amplifier is released in the form of a giant laser pulse.

laser effect: one should also set up adequate mirrors on both sides of the amplifying medium, thus creating an optical cavity. Within the latter, light waves bounce back and forth between the mirrors, each time going through the amplifying medium. The light intensity increases at each roundtrip, giving rise to the laser emission. What happens now if we insert a shutter within the cavity, thus preventing the light to bounce from mirror to mirror? The wave will no longer be able to go through the medium several times, and hence will not be amplified, so that no laser emission will be observed. Imagine at that point that you can actually control the shutter, with an "open" state (thus allowing for light circulation and amplification in the cavity), and a "closed" state (preventing light from any roundtrip in the cavity): you have now an optical gate. Assume this gate to be initially closed, while an external source continuously feeds the amplifying medium with energy. No laser action is possible since the gate is closed; however, an ever increasing number of atoms, molecules or ions get continuously excited: the potential gain of the laser increases. Imagine then that you open suddenly the shutter. The light wave is at last free to perform roundtrips in the cavity, with full benefit of the large number of atoms, ions or molecules which are excited, and hence ready to emit photons. The laser will then start abruptly, releasing all the previously stored energy into one single short and intense pulse. You could imagine photons like horses behind the starting barrier in a horse race, rushing suddenly all together when the barrier is quickly removed. In practice, you should not imagine the shutter to operate mechanically, as in standard cameras; engineers make use of quicker devices, either active optical elements, called electro-optical or acousto-optic shutters, or, passive elements, namely saturable absorbers, already described for mode-locking. In the latter case, the laser action starts automatically, when the intracavity light intensity is sufficient to bleach the saturable absorber. Finally, the funny name "Q-switch" originates from a standard practice to characterize the so-called Quality factor "Q" of cavity operation: when the shutter is closed, the quality factor is (purposefully!) very low; opening the shutter suddenly switches to a highly different "high Quality" regime of cavity operation, hence the name Q-switch.

The Q-switch method makes it far easier to trigger laser pulses, than the mode-locking technique. However, it does not allow to reach ultrashort (femtosecond) pulses, but yields pulses in the nanosecond range, which is of course much longer, since a nanosecond is one million femtoseconds. However, a nanosecond pulse lasts only few billionths of a second, still a reasonably short duration with respect to timescales from everyday life!

All these methods, which can actually be combined, open the opportunity to make flash pictures of dynamics of matter, with unprecedented
time resolution: today, we can produce flashes of light lasting just a few
femtoseconds. The identification of the first letter in the present sentence
has taken you 1,000 billion more time than that! And yet, the race goes
on to get below the one-femtosecond frontier! Physicists have resorted to
extremely sophisticated methods: they shine an intense ultrashort laser
onto a gas of atoms or molecules: the laser strips electrons off the atoms,
then accelerates them, before forcing them to slow, stop, accelerate back-
wards, and eventually have them hit the parent ion. During this recollision
process, electrons emit a tiny ultrashort flash of ultraviolet light, about five
times shorter than a femtosecond. We are stepping here into the realm of
attoseconds, one billion billion time shorter than one second, which will be
described in more detail in Chapter 4.

2.3.5. *Increasingly powerful lasers*

Concentrated in color, concentrated in time, what is next? Well, lasers also
offer a stunning concentration of power.

Lasers that supply light in a continuous way exhibit powers from few
milliwatts up to few tens of kilowatts. A laser diode delivers indeed few
milliwatts to read a compact-disc, and about 100 milliwatts to engrave it.
Argon-, or Krypton- ion lasers resort to about one watt to entertain us with
breathtaking light shows. In the high part of the continuous laser portfolio,
carbon dioxide lasers with powers of few tens of kilowatts are able to weld
metals over impressively large thicknesses.

Conversely, lasers yielding light pulses can deliver powers from few milliwatts up to petawatts, namely, millions of billions of watts. Let us start
with the lowest powers: small-scale laser diodes supply a few milliwatt light
pulses, to encode and transmit the information exchanged by phone, or over
the Internet; yttrium–aluminium garnet lasers, doped with neodymium,
deliver light pulses of few million watts, well suited to strip and clean walls
of historical monuments. Going straight to the extremes, light pulses of
about 100,000 terawatts will be obtained from the Extreme Light Infrastructure (ELI), an upcoming European infrastructure in which all the most
advanced optical technologies will be brought to their limits, and combined.
For the sake of comparison, one terawatt is 50 times the electrical power
generated by the Three Gorges dam in China; or the output power from
roughly 700 up-to-date nuclear plants! However, a nuclear plant supplies

electricity all year long, seven days a week, and around the clock; whereas an ultra-high power laser delivers such incredibly high power only once in a while, i.e., once per minute, and over extremely short periods of time, corresponding to the very short light pulse duration. Thanks to this concentration in time, a laser delivering a continuous power of 10 watts supplies a mere energy of only 10 joules in one second: this is barely sufficient to heat one gram of water by a few degrees. However, if this energy of 10 joules is now concentrated into a light flash lasting one 100th of a second, then the power reached during the pulse (known as peak power) will be increased 100-fold, and will reach one kilowatt, which would correspond to the power of any electric kettle found at home. Still with the same energy of 10 Joules, now concentrated in the amazingly short time span of 10 millionth of a billionth of a second, close to the physical limit with only four oscillations of the laser electric field, then we may reach the unbelievable power of one million billion watts, about a thousand times larger than all the electric power consumption in Europe. Attempting to create such a power but in a continuous way, would demand to have one million power plant units.

Producing such gigantic powers, even on very short times, is actually no mean feat. How can this be achieved? The principle, sketched in Figure 2.12, involves several steps. Very short pulses should first be created, as explained above, and then be amplified. However, ultrashort flashes of laser light very quickly exhibit such an enormous instantaneous power, that they would simply damage the amplifier into which a careless engineer would inject them. To prevent any damage to the amplifier, a specific technology is used, known as Chirped Pulse Amplification. In this method, the laser pulse is first stretched in time in a fully controlled and reversible way. This is achieved by splitting spatially the various colors underpinning the pulse with specific optics — diffraction gratings, then sending the color components along different paths, so that a color-dependent retardation is imposed: blue light is thus made to follow a longer path than red light. The resulting stretched pulse is much longer — typically 10,000 times longer — than the original one, so that its instantaneous power is much weaker, and it may propagate through the amplifiers without inducing any damage. Standard amplification may then take place, at the end of which the pulse is compressed back to its initial ultrashort duration, using the same method as initially, but reversing the treatments of blue and red light. In the end, the output pulse is both ultrashort and energetic, resulting in a very high instantaneous power.

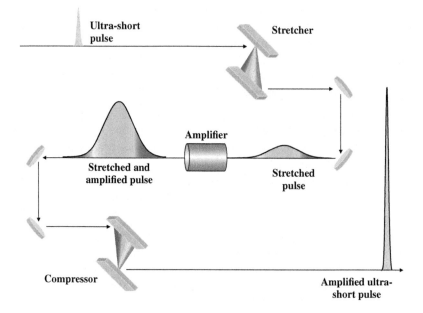

Figure 2.12: Method to amplify pulses of laser light up to extreme powers. In a first step, a laser oscillator generates a ultrashort pulse, ready to be amplified. However, its peak power would then be so high that it would damage immediately the amplifying medium. The pulse must therefore be stretched in time by inducing a "chirp", before it gets amplified, and eventually compressed back to ultrashort durations.

However, achieving such high peak powers is not the end of the story. In Chapter 1 (Section 1.4.2), we pointed out that a simple laser diode, that delivers merely 1 milliwatt of light, can be quite dangerous for the eye, although its power is much smaller than that of a standard 100-watt light bulb from home. But, in contrast with a light bulb, a laser light can be concentrated spatially over tiny areas, allowing one to reach an intensity, or power density (number of watts per squared centimeter), much higher than any classical light source. Consider this example: a helium–neon laser of 1 milliwatt, focused by an eye lens over the retina, will induce an intensity of 100 watts per squared centimeter, 1,000 times larger than the intensity produced by the sun.

Driven by their interest in observing new phenomena in extreme conditions, physicists will then seek to exploit this opportunity, and focus this outstanding light power over the tiniest possible surfaces, roughly one micrometer squared. This results in unbelievably high intensities: the ultrashort, high power laser pulses described above can then produce intensities well in excess of one thousand billion billion watts per centimeter squared. In such conditions, matter can no longer remain in the gentle solid, liquid or gaseous states of our everyday life, and by far! It turns into a plasma, very much like within stars or galaxies — a mixture of electrons, ripped off the atoms or molecules, and ions, moving at high velocities, sometimes in a totally random way, sometimes with collective behaviors. The plasma state can be thought of as an ocean of ions and electrons, which can display waves, whirls, shocks, etc. Electron waves can break out like sea waves on a coast; they can form wakes trailing behind a laser pulse going through a plasma, very much alike the water wakes observed behind speedboats at sea. Few lucky electrons may get trapped in the wake, and, imitating the craziest surfers, ride the wave, and get accelerated until they reach velocities almost equal to the speed of light. This plasma acceleration mechanism is up to 10,000 times more efficient per unit length than the most powerful conventional accelerators, based on accelerating cavities, which might be the route to particle accelerators of the future.

2.4.   Lasers: A Universal Tool?

Concentrating light in power, time, color and space... and a multitude of applications! Since their discovery, lasers have brought wildest hopes and dreams to reality. Could lasers be the solution to blast dangerous icebergs or carry high voltages? Lasers rapidly found less fanciful applications out of the lab, precisely welding and cutting matter or ablating living biological tissue as a light scalpel. Yet, lasers have not been invented in response to consumers or industrial needs. In contrast with most major innovations during the last century, such as computers that emerged in view to meet the expanding need for faster and increasingly complex computations, lasers were not invented in order to answer any specific need. However, even if nobody needed lasers at that time, lasers rapidly went on as a practical solution for a large number of scientific but also everyday problems. Let us make a brief review of some of these applications, each of them making use of the various lasers previously described in this chapter.

2.4.1.   *Cutting, welding, and cleaning*

Welding, drilling, cutting, stripping... even on very small surfaces with a record precision and on materials as hard as diamond. As shown in Figure 2.13, laser light is now regularly used to shape matter in almost any

Figure 2.13: In industry, lasers are used for various material processing needs: drilling (left), precision machining of microgears (right), but also cleaning and stripping, soldering, hardening, assembling, microlithography... (Copyright Photothèque ALPhANOV).

dimension range. On shipyards, metal sheets of more than 25 meters in length are welded thanks to laser light. In the automotive industry, lasers weld 100 times per minute. They can also sculpt matter at very small scales: like the delicate and precise pencil of a talented miniaturist, laser beams draw various motifs on matter, with a roughly 100 nm precision. If the artist pencil was so thin, his/her picture would fit on a hair!

How can we polish, dig or shape matter with a simple laser beam? One exploits the high power density that lasers deliver on very small surfaces. This tremendously localized energy produced by laser heats locally matter on a very small region, until it turns into vapor. Vaporizing materials makes it possible to cut or drill. Welding is achieved by merely heating the solder joint area: a small cylindrical zone full of metallic vapor is formed, surrounded with liquid metal; when the laser beam is turned off, the liquid metal cools down, gets solid and thus turns into the solder joint. One can also deposit very thin layers of matter thanks to laser light, a technique named "laser ablation". To deposit matter, the laser shines the matter to be deposited, which is placed in a vacuum chamber. The matter turns to vapor and deposits itself in thin layers on the target placed in the same chamber.

Depositing and etching matter... All these processes are made possible by lasers. This requires however concentrating high powers on small spots, typically up to few hundreds watts per cm^2, and therefore to focus high power lasers down to very small surfaces thanks to specific optical elements. The most widely used lasers in this field are at present carbon dioxide lasers, and sometimes solid-state lasers. The optical powers delivered vary from few watts (to cut thin sheets of acrylic glass) up to few thousands of watts (to cut 2 cm-thick metal sheets or 1 cm-thick stainless steel sheets). A machine used for such processing includes the laser source, a cutting table and a global automated system allowing one to pinpoint the impact spot of the laser onto the object to cut or drill. Various patterns can be printed (see Figure 2.13): small holes, lines, . . .

Lasers that produce light in a continuous manner constantly produce a tremendous heating. When one wishes to carve matter at very small scales, of the order of the micron (roughly 10 times smaller than the thickness of a hair), the induced local heating will generate defects; in particular the borders of the etched region will melt, forming a welding bead and collar on the edges of the carved surface due to material fusion, as can be seen in Figure 2.14 (left picture). How can we bring high powers without overheating? The solution consists in using lasers that produce ultrashort and intense flashes of light. The energy delivered by such lasers is deposited on matter solely during a very short time, avoiding any overheating of matter. Yet, during the laser pulse, the peak power is very high; one can in this way cut without heating, by literally vaporizing matter. Figure 2.14 illustrates the performance of such a technique, providing smoother etched flanks and deeper holes of ultra-small dimensions.

2.4.2. *Communicating*

Internet, mobile phones, computers. . . We are now in an "information and communication society". All these developments benefited from the

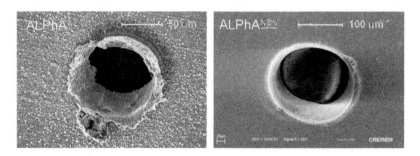

Figure 2.14: The left image shows a hole drilled in molybdenum material in a thermal regime (the laser locally heats matter) with a laser delivering nanosecond light pulses at a wavelength of 248 nm. On the right, a hole has been drilled in tungsten material in a non-thermal regime (the laser does not heat matter) with a pulsed laser producing 500 fs flashes of light at a wavelength of 1030 nm (Copyright Photothèque ALPhANOV.)

progress in the processing of microelectronic circuits with higher and higher performance and smaller size. Our computers, phones and more generally all electronic devices and equipments gather an impressive number of microchips. In order to process such increasingly smaller circuits, for instance in the manufacturing of Pentium IV processors, laser beams are used to draw each component. The laser in that case is an excimer laser emitting at a wavelength around 193 nm, in the ultraviolet.

We can process information thanks to microelectronics but we also need to store and read information. All these functionalities are made possible with lasers. Diode lasers are the core of bar codes readers, or of laser printers. Lasers also revolutionized the field of information storage, with the development of CDs and DVDs, which can record a large number of data on a very small surface (see Chapter 3 for more details).

Finally, we need to be able to share and exchange information. Again, laser light plays here a major role. The rapid expansion of telecommunications deeply and permanently changed our ways of living. To make it short, information is coded, by changing the intensity of the laser signal forming "1" (high intensity) and "0" (small intensity) bits. This information is distributed by light, which propagates along optical fibers linked to our homes. The next chapter describes in more detail the significant role of lasers in this field.

2.4.3. *Treating illnesses*

Treating your teeth, removing your tattoo, remodeling your cornea, definitively removing hair from your legs, erasing wrinkles, cauterizing blood vessels...: the laser is also a scalpel used for surgery. Thanks to its ability to concentrate light on very small surfaces, lasers can nowadays cut and cauterize biological tissues, without damaging the surrounding healthy tissues. The surgeon in ophthalmology usually employs excimer lasers to cure your myopia, the dermatologist uses a ruby laser to erase your tattoo, the dentist makes use of neodymium-doped yttrium aluminium garnet laser to treat your gingiva, while that laser, when doped with holmium instead of neodyme, can eliminate kidney stones. The first use of lasers in medicine happened in 1961 when a laser was applied to remove a tumor of the retina. Nowadays, treating with a laser has become a common technique for doctors and an almost miraculous solution for patients. The best known example is corneal surgery, that can correct myopia by remodeling the shape of the eye. Usually less invasive than classical surgery, some of the advantages of laser-assisted surgery are to reduce the risk of infection and to help healing. Chapter 7 of this book is devoted to the use of lasers in this field.

2.4.4. *Measuring*

Measuring distances, phenomena taking place on a very short time, the level of pollution... lasers can also do all that.

In order to measure distances, one exploits the directive propagation of laser light. In contrast with a flashlight, all the light carried by a laser beam propagates in space in the same direction and diverges very slightly. This is the reason why laser light is applied for elevation and alignment control when constructing roads and buildings, bridges and tunnels. For instance, laser light can be used as a plumb line when building skyscrapers. It is also exploited to measure distance in the field of telemetry. Laser light is sent onto a target that reflects it and sends it backward. Since one knows the speed of light, one can deduce the distance between the laser source and the target, by recording the time it took for a roundtrip. Very long distances can be measured using this technique. Laser light can be sent on the moon, and by collecting the few photons reflected back by mirrors placed on the lunar surface during the Apollo missions, we can know the distance between the moon and the Earth. Such measurements have shown a small moon drift away from Earth at a rate of about few centimeters per year (see Chapter 5 for more details on this topic).

In order to record phenomena of very short durations such as the ones involved in chemical reactions, one uses lasers delivering very short pulses of light. The duration of the pulses has to be smaller than the time scale of the physical mechanisms involved. These time scales are usually so short that they cannot be observed with conventional cameras. In order to make a movie of a chemical reaction which only lasts a few picoseconds (a millionth of a millionth of a second!), the lasers used deliver pulses of light with a duration 1,000 time smaller (that is femtosecond light pulses). In practice, the light pulse is divided into two; the first laser pulse triggers the chemical reaction while the second pulse, delayed with respect to the first one, takes a picture of the ongoing reaction, in the same way as a camera with a very short exposure time may take a snapshot of a race car. The movie of the reaction is then recorded by varying the time delay between the first and second pulse.

Last, in order to measure levels of pollution, the atmosphere composition or the speed of the winds, one exploits the wide spectral range (i.e., large number of colors) of femtosecond pulses. Such light pulses are sent in the atmosphere and pollutants are identified by observing the absorbed colors. When the pollutant is present, it absorbs part of the light at certain well-defined wavelengths specific of the pollutant. This will induce a decrease of the back-scattered light intensity at these colors. Ideally, different pollutants can be observed, if the laser light spectral range is wide. We already know that femtosecond pulsed lasers emit over a wide range of colors. Moreover, these pulses carry very high powers that will modify the medium in which they propagate. As a consequence, the medium will modify the speed of light at certain colors, inducing a broadening of the spectrum: the light becomes white like the one of a filament lamp, but stays directive like the laser light that produced it.

2.4.5. Supplying energy?

The NIF (National Ignition Facility) laser in California, and the Laser Mégajoule (LMJ, see Figure 2.8), currently being built next to Bordeaux, France, are both designed to reproduce fusion mechanisms at laboratory scale, similar to those that allow the sun to shine. At the core of these laser infrastructures, the two most energetic ones in the world, micropellets contain a cryogenically cooled mixture of deuterium and tritium (i.e., hydrogen nuclei with one or tho neutrons), and are compressed by converging laser or X-ray light, until their density reaches about one thousand times that of solid density matter. A central hot spot should then reach temperatures around 100 million degrees, thus inducing ignition of the fusion reactions, with which nuclei of heavy hydrogen isotopes merge to form helium nuclei, while producing roughly 100 megajoules of energy, 80 times more than the incident laser energy. In contrast with fission reactions, as used in contemporary nuclear plants, this fusion mechanism produces very little radioactive waste, since helium is a perfectly harmless gas. Moreover, sea water contains naturally huge amounts of deuterium, and tritium can be bred from lithium directly within the fusion plant. NIF and LMJ are laboratory prototypes, with a reduced number of shots per day. However, a major European project, HiPER, aims at significantly decreasing the laser energy required to ignite, and increase the laser repetition rate, thereby opening the possibility for a future fusion-based electrical power plant. Beyond being a fascinating scientific challenge, will laser fusion offer a clean and endless source of energy for mankind?

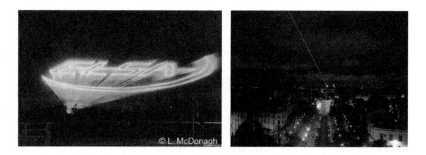

Figure 2.15: Left: Image of laser show. Right: Laser shooting between the Paris Observatory and Montmartre, used to implement an up-to-date version of the Fizeau experiment measuring the speed of light (picture by N. Treps).

2.4.6. *Entertaining*

A ballet of light pencils, lightning of building walls transcended by magic colors... Lasers also entered the world of entertainment and performing arts (see Figure 2.15). Lightning of monuments and concerts, light and sound shows, light fountains... Laser light entertains and amazes. All the colors of the palette offered by argon or solid lasers, mix to form light pictures and arabesques. Laser can even be a musical instrument with the laser harp, made of a comb of laser beams. The sound is not produced by striking the string but by stopping with one's hands the propagation of a single laser beam. When the laser beam is stopped, a music synthesizer produces the sound.

2.4.7. *Understanding*

Even though the laser has become a companion of everyday life, it still remains an essential tool of basic scientific research. Lasers have actually never left university laboratories, not only as objects of research, but also as instruments. They are used to measure light emitted or absorbed by such objects as molecules, to move atoms around, observe ultrashort processes as chemical reactions. The total list is actually way too long to be enumerated here.

Just one example: can lasers help us to explain the inner mechanism of stars? This will be one of the other challenges of the LMJ. The extreme conditions of temperature and pressure in the stellar cores can only be reproduced on Earth by means of high energy lasers. LMJ will allow one to

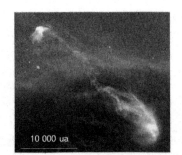

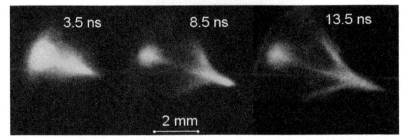

Figure 2.16: Comparison between an astrophysical jet of partially ionized gas (plasma)(top — Herbig-Haro 47, NASA photo library — Hubble Space Telescope), and a laser plasma jet (bottom) obtained with the high energy PALS laser in the Czech Republic. Equations describing these jets are very similar, with scaling laws allowing to compare phenomena occurring at very different distances (by several orders of magnitude) and very different time scales. Lasers thus permit to investigate the jets dynamics.

mimic these conditions, thereby creating a new scientific domain, laboratory astrophysics. As illustrated in Figure 2.16, galactic plasma jets can already be reproduced and studied in research laser infrastructures. How light travels within a star, or the behavior of iron in the core of a planet, are other questions to be explored by laboratory astrophysics.

2.5. Conclusion

This is the end of our introductory travel in the wide world of lasers. Lasers are diverse, in terms of size, colors, increasingly powerful and ever shorter. If lasers are diverse, so are their applications and uses: material processing, optical communications, surgery... Lasers have also become unavoidable tools used by scientists to analyze the different steps in a chemical reaction, to probe the state of a molecule... When the first operating laser was reported in 1960, it was described as "a solution in search of a problem". The laser emerged from fundamental research without answering any particular need but became a solution to an impressive number of problems. Nowadays, almost everybody has a laser at home. Yet lasers are still a research topic. In 1966, François de Closets summarized the spirit of those days: "After amazing the world, laser has still to be invented". Fifty years later, his conclusion is still relevant and appropriate.

Chapter 3

Information and Communication
Using Lasers

Mehdi Alouini

Professor,
Université de Rennes I, Institut de Physique de Rennes,
Rennes, France

Fabien Bretenaker

CNRS Senior Researcher,
Laboratoire Aimé Cotton, Orsay, France

The applications of lasers in industry are numerous. It is of course beyond the scope of this book to give an overview of these applications. Rather than trying and failing in doing so, we have chosen in this chapter to illustrate the unique properties of lasers in four different fields. The two first applications described in this chapter, namely optical telecommunications (Section 3.1) and optical information storage (Section 3.2), highlight the contribution of the spatial coherence of the laser. The third one, namely the ring laser gyroscope (Section 3.3), illustrates the amazing spectral purity that can be provided by laser light. Finally, the fourth one, known under the generic acronym LIDAR (Section 3.4), can use different laser properties, depending on its implementation. It can be based on the laser spatial coherence, the laser temporal coherence, and/or on the laser ability to emit powerful short pulses.

3.1. Lasers for Optical Telecommunications

We have forgotten today the time, yet not so far, where we communicated by telegraph. Optical telecommunications revolution took only a few years.

It came at a time when all the technological ingredients conducive to its development were there. Besides the development of low-loss optical fibers and optical amplifiers, the semiconductor laser is undoubtedly a key element in this revolution. To understand this, we must go back to 1840. That year, Samuel Finley Morse invented the telegraph which will impose, for a long time, electrical connections as the information carrier for long range links. The information carrier will remain electrical with the invention of the telephone in 1876 by Alexander Graham Bell till the first internet network in 1974 whose direct competitor was the French Minitel. At that time, transmission rates were limited to 56 kb/s, that is to say 448,000 bits per second (1 byte = 8 bits). This rate may seem high, at first glance. However, it cannot compete with the Tbit/s rates obtained today in optical telecommunication links, that is to say, one trillion bits per second!

What is a bit? Rather than carrying a signal, audio, video or other, with its original shape, the signal is digitized in binary format. In other words, it is coded in series of 1 and 0. A bit is thus the smallest unit of information that can take the value 1 or 0. For example, the binary expression of the word "laser" in the ASCII format is: 01001100 01000001 01010011 01000101 01010010. In this format, 8 bits are used to encode one letter, so 1 byte per letter. It is this arranged sequence of bits that will be conveyed. The higher the number of bits transmitted per second, the more important the amount of data transmitted per unit of time. The data rate of a link is expressed in bit/s: 1 kbit/s = 1000 bit/s, 1 Mbit/s = 1000 kbit/s, 1 Gbit/s = 1000 Mbit/s and 1 Tbit/s = 1000 Gbit/s. To give some idea, a rate of 1 Tbit/s corresponds to 10 encyclopedias of 30,000 pages or to the content of 180 CD-ROMs transmitted in 1s. This rate corresponds also to 2 million phone calls transmitted simultaneously.

At this stage, let us see how optics, and in particular the properties of laser light, makes optical broadband communications possible. In its simplest form, an optical link includes a laser, an optical fiber and a detector. The presence or absence of light on the detector corresponds respectively to a bit in the state 1 or 0. It is thus by modulating the light coming out from the laser that the information is transmitted through the fiber (see Figure 3.1). The modulation rate is nowadays done at frequencies ranging from 2.5 Gb/s up to 40 Gb/s. The information propagates in the fiber at the speed of light[1] and reaches the detector at the other end of

---

[1]In a silica fiber, the light propagates at a speed corresponding to two-thirds of its velocity in vacuum.

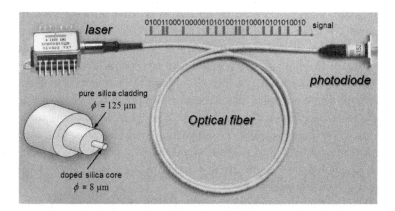

Figure 3.1: Optical link including, from left to right, a semiconductor laser, an optical fiber and a receiver. The information is encoded through a pulse sequence. Each pulse corresponds to a bit value of 1. The absence of light corresponds to the bit value 0. In this example, the pulse sequence corresponds to the word "laser" when encoded in 8 bits ASCII format. Bottom left: cross-section of a single-mode fiber. Light and the information it carries are guided in the fiber core.

the link. The most popular and high performance optical fibers consist of a 8-micron-diameter core in which the light propagates surrounded by a 125-micron-diameter cladding (see Figure 3.1). Note that the research related to the development of optical fibers was recognized in 2009 by the Nobel Prize in Physics awarded to Charles K. Kao.

Light propagation in fibers experiences some losses. The attenuation of current fibers is of about 0.2 dB/km corresponding to a diminution of the optical power by a factor of two after propagation over 15 km. However, such a very low attenuation value, which is close to the theoretical limit, is reached for a wavelength at around 1.5 μm. This is the reason why telecom lasers operate in the near infrared. For the sake of comparison, and for similar data rates, the signal would be completely attenuated in an electrical cable after a few hundred meters. Besides, the fiber transverse dimensions must be small enough in order to allow the propagation of one optical mode only. Under this condition, it is shown that the temporal spreading of the light pulses during propagation is minimized. This is all the more important as the bit rate is higher, that is light pulses are shorter and closer to each other. To meet this requirement so-called single-mode fibers whose core diameter does not exceed 8 μm are used. Obviously, such small dimensions require that enough optical power can be focused onto the fiber core. This task would be almost impossible without laser sources whose brightness far exceeds that of other types of light sources.

Although the attenuation of fibers is ridiculously small, only one thousandth of the light power reaches the detector after 150 km propagation. Thus, when the length of the telecommunication link exceeds 150 km, optical amplification is involved. An optical amplifier operates on the same principle as a laser but without mirrors. The incident photons that carry the information are duplicated through stimulated emission. Common telecom optical amplifiers can produce 10,000 photons from a single incident photon. In submarine links, these amplifiers are placed under seas and oceans every 150 to 200 km.

We have seen that a telecom laser must operate at 1.5 μm. Furthermore, it has to exhibit the highest possible brightness. But that is not all! It has also to be small. This property is undoubtedly the one that brought semiconductor lasers to revolutionize optical telecommunications. Their existence relies on the invention of heterojunctions which led to the 2000 Nobel prize awarded to Herbert Kroemer and Zhores I. Alferov. To give an order of magnitude, a telecom semiconductor laser has a length of about 500 μm and a cross-section of a few microns (see Figure 3.2). These lasers consist of a semiconductor active medium whose two ends act as the cavity mirrors. They are electrically pumped so they can be turned on and off by

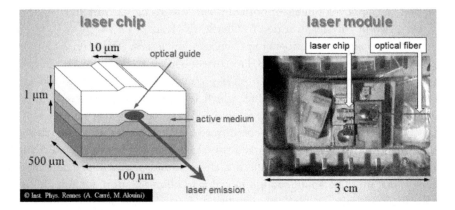

Figure 3.2: Left: Cross-section of an edge emitting semiconductor laser. Right-hand side: Integration of the laser chip in a telecom packaging. The housing contains, in addition to the laser chip, a focusing optics for fiber injection, electrical access, and a photodiode to monitor the laser power. These components are positioned on a Peltier thermoelectric cooler that regulates the laser temperature.

changing the pumping current. Doing so, an electrical sequence of bits can be converted to the same sequence of optical bits quite easily. Nevertheless, this conversion must be done at high frequencies, involving the dimensions of the laser. Indeed, the shorter the laser cavity, the faster it can be emptied or filled up with photons. Such semiconductor lasers enable producing rates of 10 Gb/s, that is, they can be turned on and off 10 billion times per second! When higher rates are required, one makes use of an external intensity modulator that follows a continuous laser.

Telecom lasers naturally oscillate at several wavelengths. In this case, the laser is called multimode. As the different wavelengths do not travel at the same speed in the fiber, the optical pulses carrying the information suffer temporal spreading and eventually interleave at the output leading to a degradation of the transmitted information. This spread is particularly problematic as the pulses become short, close to each other, and have to travel long distances. This is why multimode lasers are used when the targeted bit rate is low or when the optical link is short. Conversely, when the link is long and the bit rate is high, it is essential to use a single wavelength laser. Such laser is called single mode, as already explained in Chapter 1. Single-frequency operation is obtained by etching on the active medium along the propagation axis an optical grating that fosters the oscillation of one wavelength to the detriment of the others. Semiconductor lasers are mounted in a housing of a few cm^3 including the optical components for injection into the fiber, electrical access networks, temperature and optical power control components (see Figure 3.2).

The steady increase of data rates led to further constraints on the laser. Indeed, they have to deliver high optical powers. In order to understand, one has to go back to the pulse train and focus on its detection at the link output. The detection device must be able to distinguish between the two bits 1 and 0. To this aim, the pulse must carry a number of photons higher than a threshold given by the detector quality. However, increasing the data rate is accompanied by a reduction of the pulse width and brings the pulses closer to each other. As the number of photons per pulse must remain higher than the detection threshold, on the one hand, and the number of pulses per time unit is increased, on the other hand, the number of photons per time unit must increase. It is in this way that the optical power delivered by telecommunication semiconductor lasers has increased gradually from few hundred microwatts up to 20 or even to 50 milliwatts today.

At this point, one may wonder how to take advantage of the high speed of a telecom laser while a phone conversation, for example, requires only a

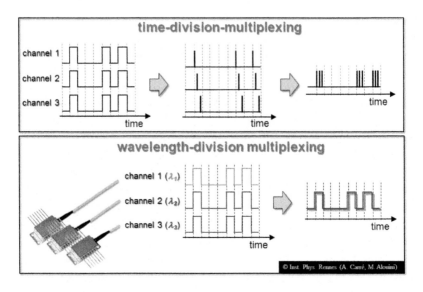

Figure 3.3:   Principle of time division and wavelength multiplexing. Time division multiplexing consists in interleaving in the time domain the pulse trains coming from each channel. By contrast, for wavelength multiplexing, the pulse trains of the different channels can overlap in the time domain and spatially provided that each channel has its own wavelength. In this case, it is the optical spectra that should not overlap.

rate of 56 kb/s. The technique of *time division multiplexing* is implemented. Let us consider for example three phone conversations. Suppose that each conversation requires 100,000 pulses per second. It is possible to compress the pulses and to interleave them in the time domain so that the final pulse train includes 300,000 pulses per second (see Figure 3.3). This can be repeated as many times as necessary until reaching the bit rate of a telecom laser, namely 10 billion pulses per second. The reverse operation consisting in untangling the different phone conversations at the link output is called *time division demultiplexing*.

Although the pulse rate at the laser output is of the order of tens of Gb/s, it is possible to go much further to reach transmission rates of the order of the Tbit/s, that is, a hundred times faster. To this aim, a second technique called *wavelength division multiplexing* is used. It is based on the property of white light decomposition. We all know since Newton that white light is composed of rainbow's colors. These colors can be separated and recombined back to form white light. Thus, let us consider three signals to transmit, each one at a rate of 10 Gbit/s. Rather than sending theses signals one after another, which would take three times longer, on can send them in parallel using three lasers whose wavelengths are slightly different from each other (see Figure 3.3). These three different wavelengths are then focused into the link fiber. One then obtains along the fiber core three pulse trains at 10 Gbit/s which are superimposed in time, but each pulse train and therefore each signal has its own wavelength. After propagation in the fiber, the three wavelengths are separated before detection, which allows us to acquire independently each signal. This operation is called wavelength division demultiplexing. Wavelength division multiplexing uses a fundamental property of the light that permits, to some extent, to make many photons overlap in space and time without interacting together. Let us mention that this technique is that used in the radio wave domain to convey simultaneously many different radio stations, each one being tuned to a specific frequency. In our example, wavelength division multiplexing has allowed us to achieve a transmission rate of 30 Gbit/s from three lasers each one producing a 10 Gbit/s rate. In practice, a hundred wavelengths can be multiplexed in a single fiber. The set of these wavelengths forms a comb covering the spectral range 1530 to 1570 nm and whose teeth are spaced by 0.4 nm. Wavelength division multiplexing requires therefore the lasers to be single mode and stable in terms of wavelength. Indeed, their wavelengths should not drift more than 0.01 nm in order to avoid any interleave of the different communication channels. Again, the coherence property of laser light enables to tackle this constraint.

Where do we stand today? The fiber link global network is increasing inexorably. This network spans in millions of kilometers of cables considering only underwater and terrestrial transcontinental links. These are real information highways through which the main part of global information travels, from phone conversations to internet videos. Nothing seems to stop the mad rush of information since transmission rate records are announced almost every month. Today we are hearing about tens of Tbit/s in a single fiber. Internet service providers offer fiber to the home. We come to the era where the light as information carrier enters our homes after having conquered continents. Obviously, the proposed optical links between the internet node and the subscriber are much less efficient than those described above for long haul optical communication. Nevertheless, owing to their data rates of 100 Mbits/s, their performances still remain well above common electrical connections. Along with this frantic race to high data rates, one sees the advent of free space optical links between buildings. In this case, the light and the information it carries no longer propagate through a fiber but directly through air. For such free space links, advantage is taken of the high directivity property of laser beams. These lasers that amaze us still have a bright future ahead of them.

3.2. Lasers for Optical Storage

The need of information storage has never been felt as much as in the recent years. While paper has remained essential for centuries, one witnesses in recent decades a digital revolution. Texts, paintings, photos, videos, music are stored in digital format on media whose sizes are decreasing while their storage capacities are increasing. Among the storage methods that have revolutionized our way of life, the most noteworthy ones are magnetic storage, optical storage, and more recently flash memories. We shall limit ourselves here to a description of optical storage principles with a focus on its key element: the laser.

Before getting into the heart of the matter, let us linger for a while on how the information is coded. Not too long ago, we made do with recording on a medium an exact replica of the signal. To record music for example, a groove with varying depth was etched on a vinyl disc. To capture a scene, a series of picture-shots was printed on a silver film and then scrolled to reproduce back the action. This approach does not guarantee a good reproduction quality. In addition, the type of medium used depended on the type of data to record. Today, all the information under consideration, namely video, audio, or else, are systematically converted to binary format which corresponds to a sequence of bits of values 1 or 0. It is this sequence of bits that is stored on a digital medium. The storage capacity of media is expressed in bytes: $1\,kB = 1000$ bytes, $1\,MB = 1000\,kB$, $1\,GB = 1000\,MB$ and $1\,TB = 1000\,GB$.

The first optical storage medium having flooded the market is the audio Compact Disc (CD) launched by Sony and Philips in 1982. The CD is a wafer made of plastic material on which are engraved tiny pits associated to the digital signal (see Figure 3.4). These pits are arranged along a track spiraling out from the center of the disc. The surface of the disc is entirely coated by a thin reflective metal layer. To read data, a laser beam is focused on the track as the track scrolls. The light is more or less reflected towards a detector that converts the light signal into an electrical signal (see Figure 3.4). As opposed to what one might think, a pit does not correspond to a given bit state 1 or 0. Actually, it is the step

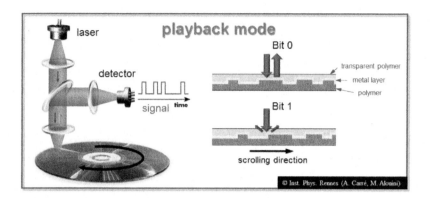

Figure 3.4: Operation principle of a CD player. During the rotation of the disc, the laser beam probes the track with the pits scrolling. The step corresponding to a transition from a pit to a plateau, or from a plateau to a pit, leads to a destructive interference which cancels the reflected beam in the detector direction. The detector assigns the associated decrease of optical power to the bit value 1. When the beam is perfectly reflected to the detector direction the bit value is assigned to 0.

corresponding to the transition from a plateau to a pit or from a pit to a plateau that is associated to the bit 1. In between two steps, either a pit or a plateau, the bit value is set to 0. To understand the reason of this, one must remember the principle of interferences between two monochromatic waves. During a step transition between a pit and a plateau part of the illumination beam is reflected by the pit whereas the other part is reflected by the plateau. The depth of the step is calculated so that the two parts of the reflected light interfere destructively. As a result, the detector receives a tiny amount of light which is associated to a bit value of 1 (see Figure 3.4). In contrast, everywhere else the light does not interfere destructively and is totally reflected back to the detector. A high amount of light is associated to a bit value of 0. Obviously, this principle of light interference operates because the light is monochromatic, justifying the use of a laser.

The choice of a laser source is also ruled by the need of increasing storage capacity. Indeed, the smaller the size of the pits, the narrower the tracks, and the higher the recorded data density. However, when the laser beam is focused, the light spot dimensions must not exceed the lateral size of one pit. It is the peculiar spatial properties of the laser beam that are exploited here to obtain a light spot whose diameter is in the micrometer range. Thus, the pits of a CD-ROM are only 0.6 microns, allowing to engrave and to roll-around a 5-km-long data track over 22,000 rounds. In general, the storage capacity of the medium is limited by the laser spot size. Moreover, there is a fundamental principle in optics that forbids focusing a light beam to a size much smaller than its wavelength. Accordingly, it is increasingly common to shorten the wavelength of the lasers that are used for optical storage. In the case of a CD-ROM, the reading laser operates at 780 nm, i.e., in the very near infrared, providing a storage capacity of about 700 MB. In the case of a Digital Video Disc (DVD), the reading laser operates at 635 nm, that is, in the red. A storage capacity of 4.7 GB is then reached on a disc whose area is the same that of a CD-ROM. It was only in 1996 that Shuji Nakamura succeeded in developing the eagerly awaited blue semiconductor laser. This laser oscillating at 405 nm will lead, a few years later, to the development of the Blu-ray standard. This standard, which has now entered our homes, offers a storage capacity of 27 GB, that is, five times that of a DVD (see Figure 3.5).

Apart from reading, lasers are also used to record data on rewritable discs. In this case, the data is not engraved mechanically as a series of pits, but engraved optically in a photosensitive layer whose optical transmission varies according to the applied power. The metallic layer which reflects the light is, this time, positioned underneath the photosensitive layer. As a result, bit 1 corresponds now to an absorbing area of the photosensitive layer, whereas bit 0 corresponds to a transparent area. In order to make the photosensitive material absorb, it is necessary to briefly bring its

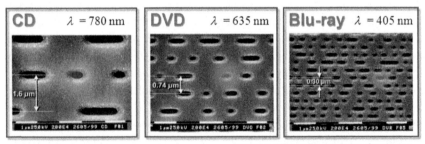

Source : jean-philippe muller - http://www.ta-formation.com/

Figure 3.5:   Views of the engraved surface of a CD, a DVD and a Blu-ray disc. The shorter the wavelength, the smaller the laser spot is after focusing. Decreasing the wavelength enables to increase the density of coding elements (pits) per unit area and, therefore, to increase the storage capacity of the medium. Obviously, obtaining a small spot size is achieved at the cost of using also high aperture lenses.

temperature above 500°C. Consequently, the laser must provide a power of about 15 mW on a tiny area of the tenth of μm^2. In a rewritable disc, this change of state is reversible. Indeed, the photosensitive layer returns back to its initial state of transparency by bringing it briefly to 200°C. The required optical power is then 5 mW only.

In addition to storage capacity, recording speed and data access are important parameters. Regarding the recording, its speed is ensured by the small dimensions of the semiconductor laser. Indeed, as mentioned in the section related to optical communications, the small size of the laser cavity in conjunction with the electrical pumping enables to modulate the light at very high frequencies. For example, the etching rate of a rewritable DVD reaches today 10 MB/s, which corresponds to a data transfer rate of 80 Mbit/s. However, this comes at a price. The more the recording speed is increased the more powerful the laser must be because the available time to burn one bit becomes shorter. As a result, engraving lasers produce today pulses whose peak powers are of the order of 250 mW.

Among the optical storage techniques, there is one powerful approach, although less present in general public applications because of its high cost. It is the magneto-optic recording technique (see Figure 3.6) which emerged in the 1980s. By combining the strengths of optical and magnetic technologies, it offers higher storage capacity as compared to purely optical

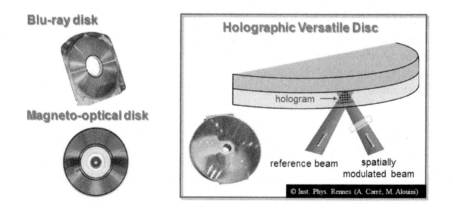

Figure 3.6:   Right-hand side: Holographic disc. Unlike other types of media such as the two examples in the left-hand side of the figure, the data are engraved in the three dimensions of the photosensitive layer. The storage capacity of a holographic disc is of the order of one TB, which corresponds to the storage capacity of 40 Blu-ray discs.

techniques. The disc is covered with a magnetic alloy sensitive to light. Bits 0 and 1 are encoded on the medium as two different magnetic orientations. As for the purely optical technology, reading is performed with a laser. When the track is scrolled, the polarization[2] state of the reflected laser beam changes according to the magnetic orientation associated to each bit. Then, this change of polarization is detected and converted to an electrical signal. Data writing, in turn, is achieved with a magnetic head, but is assisted by a laser which locally heats up the magnetic layer in order to enable or disable the change of magnetic state. Magneto-optic discs offer the advantage of being sensitive neither to temperature nor to magnetic disturbances that can damage or destroy information in the case of a purely magnetic disc.

Finally, it is important to mention the holographic data storage technology (see Figure 3.6). It came into existence three years ago with the Holographic Versatile Disc (HVD). It relies on coherence properties of laser radiation. Basically, holographic storage consists in recording the information within a photosensitive polymer using, this time, two laser beams that intersect. Without going into details, this approach enables to encode bits both on the surface and in the volume of the medium. In other words, a pattern consisting of bright and dark points is created in the three dimensions inside the photosensitive layer. This pattern is obtained due to the interferences occurring between the two laser beams. The storage capacity is thus significantly increased. The first HVDs that appeared recently on the market provide a storage capacity as high as 300 GB, and we are already hearing about TB capacities, that is to say, 1000 GB. At the same time, significant research efforts are currently directed towards optical storage in molecular materials. Here again, one takes advantage of the laser beam properties to switch the molecule from one state to the other, each state corresponding to a bit value.

3.3.   The Ring Laser Gyroscope

As early as the 1960's, the laser has found applications in the domain of inertial navigation. In order to reach its destination, a vehicle such as, e.g., a plane, needs to know its position and orientation in space (heading, attitude, etc.) at every moment. To this aim, one can show that the kinematic

---

[2]The polarization of light refers to the direction along which the vibrating electric field of the optical wave is aligned.

equations of the vehicle motion can be integrated provided (i) one knows the initial position of the aircraft and (ii) one measures all along the trip the accelerations and angular velocities of the vehicle along three rectangular axes. This is why an inertial measurement unit generally contains three accelerometers (which measure the three accelerations along three axes) and three gyrometers (which measure the three angular velocities around these three axes). To reach a precision in positioning of the order of one nautical mile per hour (leading for example to a positioning error of a few miles after a trip from Paris to New York), one can calculate that the drift of the gyrometers must not exceed typically 0.01°/h (degree per hour), i.e., one thousandth of the earth rotation rate!

Different physical effects can be used to measure the rotation rate of a vehicle. For example, mechanical gyroscopes are well-known sensors. Light also provides a way to sense rotations. The effect on which optical gyroscopes are based is the Sagnac effect, named after the French physicist who demonstrated it experimentally as early as 1913. Its principle can be easily understood thanks to Figure 3.7. One indeed considers a closed path, that we will take circular for the sake of simplicity. Light is launched inside this path along the two propagation directions, starting at initial time $t = 0$ from a beamsplitter located at point O (see Figure 3.7(a)). If the system is at rest, the time taken by light to travel along one roundtrip and come back to O is $T = L/c = 2\pi R/c$ where L is the perimeter of the circular path of radius R and c the velocity of light. On the contrary, if the system rotates at angular velocity Ω around an axis perpendicular to the interferometer plane, then Figure 3.7(b) shows that the distance traveled

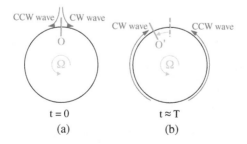

CCW wave / CW wave
O
Ω
t = 0
(a)

CW wave / CCW wave
O'
Ω
t ≈ T
(b)

Figure 3.7: Principle of the Sagnac effect. (a) Starting from a beamsplitter initially located in O, one injects light in the two opposite directions along a circular path rotating at angular velocity Ω. (b) Because of rotation, the duration of the trip is not the same for the clockwise (CW) and counter-clockwise (CCW) propagation directions.

by light to reach the beamsplitter will be different for the two directions of propagation. Indeed, during time T, this beamsplitter will move from O to point O', corresponding to a rotation angle ΩT (see Figure 3.7(b)). The lengths L_{ccw} and L_{cw} traveled by light in the two propagation directions thus exhibit a difference given by:

$$L_{ccw} - L_{cw} \simeq 2R\Omega T = 4\pi R^2 \Omega / c, \qquad (3.1)$$

which creates a phase shift equal to $\Delta\phi = 2\pi(L_{ccw} - L_{cw})/\lambda$ between these waves, where λ is the wavelength of the considered light. Consequently, to detect rotation rates equal to 0.01 °/h with a Sagnac interferometer of radius $R = 0.1$ m operating at visible wavelengths, one needs to be able to measure phase shifts much smaller than 1 nanoradian, i.e., smaller than 10^{-16} times the phase accumulated by one wave during its roundtrip in the interferometer.

One way to measure such small phase shifts consists in using a "ring" laser instead of a Sagnac interferometer. Such a ring laser is sketched in Figure 3.8. Inside such a ring laser cavity, light can travel along two opposite directions of propagation. When the cavity plane rotates at angular velocity Ω, the effective lengths of the cavity in the two directions are different, with a difference given by Equation (3.1). As seen in Chapter 1, the wavelength of light must be resonant inside the cavity in which it oscillates, meaning that the wavelength of the laser light must be equal to the optical

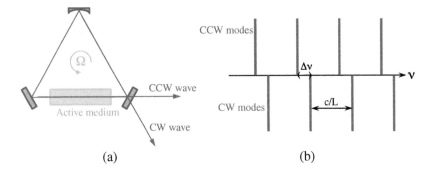

(a)   (b)

Figure 3.8: Principle of the ring laser gyroscope. (a) One builds a ring laser, using for example a triangular cavity, thus sustaining oscillation of one CCW mode and one CW mode. (b) Because of the rotation of the laser at angular velocity Ω, the Sagnac effect shifts the two frequencies of the laser corresponding to the two propagation directions by a quantity $\Delta\nu$. This frequency difference is measured by measuring the beatnote obtained when the two counterpropagating beams are recombined at the output of the laser.

length of the cavity divided by an integer number. Since $L_{ccw} \neq L_{cw}$, the eigenfrequencies of the cavity (i.e., the frequencies of the successive longitudinal modes) are different for the two propagation directions, as shown in Figure 3.8(b). The frequency difference induced by rotation thanks to the Sagnac effect is given by:

$$\Delta \nu = \frac{4A}{\lambda L}\Omega, \qquad (3.2)$$

where A is the area of the cavity, L its perimeter, and λ the wavelength of the laser light. To measure a rotation, one thus just needs to recombine the two beams at the output of the laser and to measure their beatnote frequency $\Delta \nu$. The quantity $K = \frac{4A}{\lambda L}$ is called the scale factor of the ring laser gyro. For example, for a ring cavity exhibiting a 30-cm-perimeter and $\lambda = 633$ nm, one gets $K \simeq 0.5$ Hz/(°/h). Thus, to be able to measure angular velocities as small as 0.01°/h, as required by inertial navigation needs, one must be able to measure variations of the two optical frequencies of a few millihertz, i.e., relative variations of the order of 10^{-17}!

Many technological issues must be dealt with before one is able to reach such a sensitivity. The most intricate one is the lock-in region. The red line in Figure 3.9 reproduces the ideal response of the ring laser gyroscope, as given by Equation (3.2): the frequency difference between the two waves is proportional to the angular velocity. However, for small angular velocities, one experimentally observes that the two frequencies remain locked. The response of the sensor is then given by the blue line: the system is blind

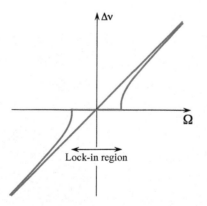

Figure 3.9: Evolution of the ring laser gyroscope beatnote frequency $\Delta \nu$ versus angular frequency Ω. The red line is the ideal linear response given by Equation (3.2). The blue line exhibits a lock-in region for small rotation rates. Inside this lock-in region, the two optical frequencies are locked.

at small rotation rates! This lock-in phenomenon is due to the coupling phenomena between the two waves. It is similar to the synchronization between two clocks exchanging energy observed by Christian Huygens during the 17th century. In the ring laser gyroscope, the frequencies of the two waves can lock because of the light backscattered from one wave into the other by the defects of the cavity mirrors. This effect has triggered significant technological developments aiming at improving the quality of mirrors. Many other fields have benefited from these developments such as, e.g., the interferometers aiming at detecting gravitational waves (see Chapter 5) or the ultrastable cavities on the resonances of which metrological lasers are locked. However, even with mirrors built using up-to-date technologies, the lock-in region remains of the order of a few tens or hundreds of °/h, i.e., at least 1000 times too large. To circumvent this problem, one applies a zero-mean sinusoidal rotation rate to the ring laser gyroscope (known as the "dither"), maintaining the system out of the lock-in region during the largest part of time.

Commercial ring laser gyroscopes are helium–neon lasers (see Chapter 2). Their cavities are machined out of vitro-ceramic materials exhibiting extremely small thermal expansion coefficients and ensuring the mandatory thermal and mechanical stability. This allows them to operate in hostile environments such as military airplanes, missiles, or spatial launchers. Figure 3.10 represents two examples of such ring laser gyroscopes: one, on the left, based on a triangular cavity and a *three axis* ring laser gyro on the right. The latter one is constituted of three ring laser gyroscopes with

Figure 3.10:   Left: Helium–neon ring laser gyroscope based on a triangular cavity. Right: The PiXYZ 22, a three-axis ring laser gyroscope. Copyright Thales/ photos Etienne Bonnaudet and Patrick Darphin.

cavities perpendicular to three perpendicular spatial directions. It allows to measure the three rotation rates with a single sensor.

Nowadays, one uses ring laser gyroscopes in many civilian and military systems: military combat and non-combat aircrafts, helicopters, missiles, ships, terrestrial vehicles, space launchers, etc. All this has been made possible by the extraordinary coherence properties of laser light!

3.4. The LIDAR

Sometimes referred to as LASER-RADARs, LIDARs are the equivalent of RADARs in the optical domain. While RADAR holds for *RAdio Detection And Ranging*, LIDAR means *LIght Detection And Ranging*. The basic principle of LIDARs is the same as the one of RADARs: one launches a light pulse which is elastically or inelastically backscattered by a target (cloud, aerosols, atmosphere, solid target, etc.). One then analyzes the properties (intensity, time delay, polarization, frequency spectrum, etc.) of this backscattered radiation in order to remotely obtain informations on the target (shape, velocity, distance, concentration of chemical or biological species, temperature, pressure, etc.). The applications of LIDARs, as well civilian as military, are countless. Here, we have selected two of them, which deal with environmental applications: the atmospheric LIDAR based on aerosol detection and the wind LIDAR.

3.4.1. *The aerosol LIDAR*

Figure 3.11 presents the principle of such a LIDAR. A pulsed laser emits light pulses with a duration of a few nanoseconds (see the description of the operation of such so-called "Q-switched lasers" in Chapter 2). A small part of the emitted light is scattered[3] by small particles present in the atmosphere such as aerosols, water droplets and crystals located in clouds, dust and smoke particles, etc. The fraction of this scattered light that goes back in the direction of the source is called the *backscattered* light. Since this scattering is more efficient for short wavelengths than for long wavelengths, one uses lasers emitting in the ultraviolet part of the electromagnetic spectrum (Nd:YAG laser emitting at 1064 nm which is frequency tripled to lead to light emission at 355 nm). The excellent directivity of the laser, together

---

[3]Scattered light is light which is redirected in all directions, like day light is scattered by water particles on foggy days or like light is scattered by a glass of milk.

Figure 3.11: Left: Principle of operation of a LIDAR. Right: Example of an aerosol LIDAR settled in Namibia. Copyright Leosphere.

with the use of a telescope to collimate the laser beam, permits to perfectly control which cone of the sky is shone at a given moment.

One part of the light backscattered by the atmosphere is collected by a telescope, spectrally filtered, and detected. One then obtains a signal which evolves versus time like the one of Figure 3.12. This signal is plotted as a function of the delay multiplied by half the velocity of light, i.e., as a function of the distance to the backscattering source. Moreover, the signal itself has been multiplied by the square of this distance to compensate for the natural spreading of light during its propagation. Such a signal thus directly provides a map of the scattering versus altitude along the LIDAR aiming line. For example, one clearly sees a step for an altitude of 2,200 meters, which corresponds to the end of the atmospheric limit layer containing the most part of aerosols. The residual scattering above this altitude mainly comes from atmospheric molecules (N_2, O_2). The signal at about 11,000 meters corresponds to a high altitude cloud (cirrus cloud). The evolution of this signal versus time is coded in false colors in the plot at the top of Figure 3.12, over a duration of almost 5.5 hours. The excellent directivity of the laser allows one to distinguish the clouds passing by at a given location, to measure the evolution of the limit layer. These data contribute to the understanding of the climate and to weather forecasts.

Figure 3.13 illustrates some other applications of the same system. The left figure shows, over a few hour time duration, the passage at high altitude

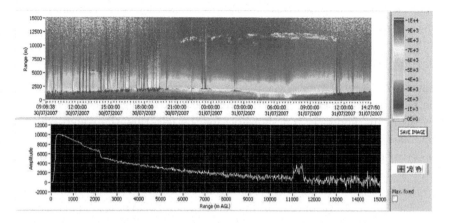

Figure 3.12: Bottom figure: Evolution of the detected intensity multiplied by the square of the propagation distance as a function of the delay after emission of the pulse multiplied by half the velocity of light. The top image reproduces a section of the sky versus time. One can clearly distinguish the atmospheric limit layer (up to 1,000 to 2,000 meters) and the occurrence of high altitude clouds at 10,000 to 20,000 meters. Copyright Leosphere.

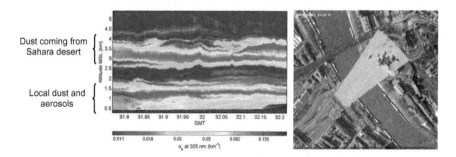

Figure 3.13: Left figure: Dust particle cloud coming from the Sahara desert and flying over Orsay, France, at about 3 to 4 km altitude. The usual aerosol layer is located at an altitude of about 2 km. The figure on the right has been obtained by scanning the LIDAR horizontally just above the ground level. One can perfectly see the spatial distribution of pollutants emitted by cars in the vicinity of the exit of the tunnel below the Fourvière hill in Lyon, France. Copyright P. Chazette, LSCE/CEA and Leosphere.

over the Paris area of a cloud of sand dust coming from Sahara. The right figure has been performed in Lyon, France, by horizontally scanning the LIDAR in a horizontal plane. One can precisely follow the density and spatial distribution of pollutants emitted by cars and other ground vehicles, where and how they are emitted, and how they are dispersed in the environment.

3.4.2. *The Doppler LIDAR*

Some other applications of the LIDAR are based on the Doppler effect. Let us recall that this effect shifts the frequency of the light that is reflected by a moving body. It is responsible for the fact that the sound emitted by a fast ambulance changes pitch when the ambulance moves towards the observer or away from him. The same thing happens for light: depending on whether the object that has scattered light is moving towards or away from the detector, the light frequency is increased or decreased, respectively.

The principle of operation of the Doppler LIDAR is schematized in Figure 3.14(a). This time, the laser has a wavelength equal to 1.5 μm and the pulse duration is of the order of 200 ns in order to achieve a spectral resolution good enough to precisely determine the wind velocity. Indeed, the pulse duration must be long enough to contain a number of optical periods allowing a precise determination of the frequency. The light backscattered by moving aerosols is frequency shifted by a quantity proportional to the projection of the velocity vector along the laser beam. In order to reconstruct the velocity vector of these aerosols, one scans the emission direction of the LIDAR as shown in Figure 3.14(b). By using a scan amplitude of the order of 30° and pulse durations of the order of 200 ns with a 20 kHz

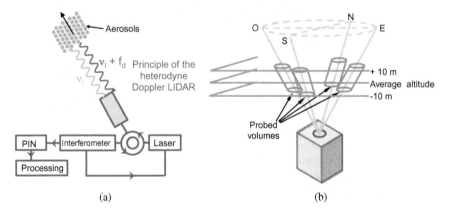

(a)   (b)

Figure 3.14:   (a) Principle of the Doppler LIDAR. The signal backscattered by moving aerosols is frequency shifted by a quantity f_d due to the Doppler effect. (b) Principle of the measurement along four directions to reconstruct the vectorial velocity field. Copyright Leosphere.

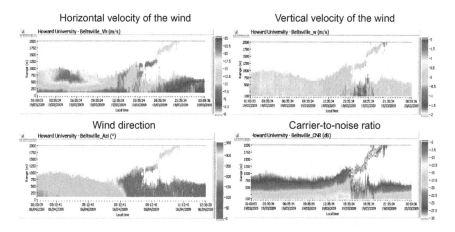

Figure 3.15: Measurement of several wind parameters during a few hours at an altitude of several hundreds of meters. In each plot, the horizontal axis holds for the time and the vertical axis for the altitude. The two upper figures correspond to the horizontal and vertical components of the wind velocity, respectively. The amplitude of these velocity components are coded in false colors. The lower left figure plots, also in false colors, the orientation of the horizontal component of the wind. It illustrates the fact that this LIDAR provides in real time the modulus and direction of the wind velocity for all altitudes along the laser beam direction. Copyright Leosphere.

Figure 3.16: A wind LIDAR probing the wind in the vicinity of a wind farm. Copyright Leosphere.

repetition rate, one succeeds in measuring the velocity vector corresponding to a 20-m-thick layer with an altitude range of the order of 200 m.

One very important application of this Doppler LIDAR consists in mapping the wind velocity field in order to optimize the choice of the location of wind farms. Indeed, in order to perform this optimization, one needs to remotely measure many characteristics of the wind velocity field: vertical profile, velocity amplitude and direction maps, measurement of shear forces and turbulences at any altitude up to 200 m (See Figures 3.15 and 3.16).

3.5. Conclusion

As mentioned in the introduction to this chapter, the different laser applications use the different characteristics of this unique light source. For example, the laser spectral purity is used in the ring laser gyroscope and the Doppler LIDAR. The possibility to concentrate a large light energy in a small duration pulse is used in telecommunication applications and in different kinds of LIDARs. Finally, the possibility to concentrate all the emitted light on a few square-micron-surface (one says that the beam quality is diffraction-limited) has been instrumental in the development of optical information storage technologies and in the LIDAR again (spatial directivity).

All these possibilities come from the fact that a laser is a source of light able to put a huge number of photons (typically 10^{12} photons) in the same mode of the electromagnetic field, contrary to "classical" sources which, although quite powerful, are never able to put more than a fraction of a photon in the same mode of the field. The laser applications discussed in the other chapters of this book (see Chapters 4, 5, 6, and 7) have also been successful thanks to this unique feature of laser light.

Chapter 4

Ultrashort Light Sources

Nicolas Forget

Researcher, Fastlite, Orsay, France

Manuel Joffre

CNRS Senior Researcher,
Laboratoire d'Optique et Biosciences,
Ecole Polytechnique, Palaiseau, France

Thierry Ruchon

CEA Researcher, IRAMIS/SPAM, Saclay, France

4.1. Introduction

One of the most remarkable properties of lasers is their ability to operate in pulsed mode, i.e., to emit light during short periods of time. Some laser pulses are so brief that they are qualified of ultrashort and that the relevant sub-unit of measurement is the femtosecond (10^{-15} s): one millionth of a billionth of a second. In 2014, the shortest pulses ever produced even have a duration shorter than a hundred attoseconds, or 10^{-17} s (an attosecond, denoted as *as*, equals 10^{-18} s). Far from being purely speculative, this race towards the shortest pulses is driven by numerous practical applications, both scientific and commercial. A first application field is naturally the observation of ultrafast phenomena. Just as a flash that can "freeze" a fast motion, ultrashort pulses can be used to observe transient phenomena whose time constants are in the range of 10^{-10} to 10^{-15} s, which is typical of atomic motion in solids, and of chemical or biochemical reactions.

A second field of applications originates from the high electric field associated with ultrashort pulses. In optics as in electronics, the power is defined as the amount of energy delivered per unit of time. For a constant amount of energy, an optical pulse is therefore all the more intense that it is shorter. Consequently, an ultrashort pulse is also most often ultra-intense. As an example, an optical pulse with an energy of $100\,\mu$J and a duration of $20\,$fs corresponds to a peak power of $5\,$GW, which is equivalent to the combined electrical outputs of a few nuclear power plants. When such a laser beam is focused, the peak electric field is intense enough to overcome the electrostatic force which binds electrons to the nucleus in atoms, and hence to induce ionization (i.e., to pull some electrons out of the atom). It is of course possible to achieve the same result with longer laser pulses but at the cost of much higher energy. Furthermore, ultrashort laser pulses induce ionization on a time scale which is much shorter than what is required for heat to propagate in solids. A key industrial application of ultrashort sources is therefore athermal ablation: contactless and "cold" cutting or drilling (see Section 4.2, especially Figure 2.14). These properties are especially valuable for flammable materials and for medical applications (ophthalmic surgery for example, see Section 4.7).

Even with much smaller energies, the electric field of ultrashort pulses is strong enough to induce dramatic effects in most materials. These so-called nonlinear effects have found many spectacular applications. One example is nonlinear microscopy, an imaging technique used to reveal three-dimensional intra- or extracellular structures in intact biological tissues, or even *in vivo*. Nonlinear optics also offers means to extend the spectral range of the *primary* laser sources which are mostly concentrated in the near infrared. For example, harmonic generation is a nonlinear process allowing to produce electromagnetic radiation whose frequencies are integer multiples of the initial frequency. Starting from an infrared femtosecond laser, it is thus possible to generate ultraviolet (UV) or even X-ray pulses, as will be discussed at the end of this chapter.

Last, femtosecond lasers exhibit broad spectra, which means that they consist of a combination of many different optical frequencies. This feature is of particular interest for optical coherent tomography, another biomedical imaging method developed in the last 20 years and described in Chapter 7. In addition, these frequencies are automatically organized in perfectly regular combs. This unique property triggered a significative breakthrough in time and frequency metrology, as discussed in Chapter 5.

4.2. Time and Frequency

A femtosecond laser is primarily a laser, such as those described in the rest of this book, and therefore consists of a cavity in which a gain medium is inserted in order to compensate for optical losses. Let L be the length of the cavity and T the time needed for light to propagate along one roundtrip. If we first assume the cavity to be empty, L and T are related by $T = 2L/c$, where c is the speed of light in vacuum. As we have seen in Chapter 1, there is a closing relationship for the electric field propagating in the cavity which requires that the electric field makes an integer number of oscillations during the period T. By definition, the number of oscillations made by a field oscillating at frequency ν within a time interval T is equal to the product νT. We can therefore deduce the relationship $\nu T = n$, where n is an integer characterizing the longitudinal mode considered. The longitudinal modes (i.e., the frequencies allowed to propagate within the cavity) are thus defined by $\nu_n = n/T$ and are naturally equidistant. In a single-frequency laser, particularly valuable for its spectral purity, a single longitudinal mode is selected. In a femtosecond laser, we will show that the goal is exactly the opposite: it is instead desirable to sustain the simultaneous and concerted oscillations of a large number of longitudinal modes.

Let us first consider what happens when two consecutive longitudinal modes of a laser, ν_n and ν_{n+1}, are superimposed, as shown in Figure 4.1(a). Because the two modes do not have exactly the same frequency, the modes are sometime in phase (dash-dotted vertical line), resulting in a maximum total intensity, and sometimes in antiphase (solid vertical line), resulting in a vanishing total intensity. This produces what is called a beat, or, in other words, a periodic modulation of the light intensity. This very general phenomenon occurs, for example, when two music instruments are slightly detuned with respect to each other, which creates an unpleasant sound beating. In the case of lasers, the beat period is equal to the roundtrip period T since $\nu_{n+1}T - \nu_n T = 1$.

This time beating is already a pulse embryo, even though the corresponding pulse *duration* remains quite long. To get shorter pulses, one must increase the number of contributing modes. As shown in Figures 4.1(b) and 4.1(c), the greater the number of modes, the shorter the time range where the modes add up constructively. It can be seen that on the sides of the produced pulse (limit of the shaded area), there is a time shift of half an oscillation period between the central mode and the edge mode. How does this time shift translate in terms of frequencies of the modes involved?

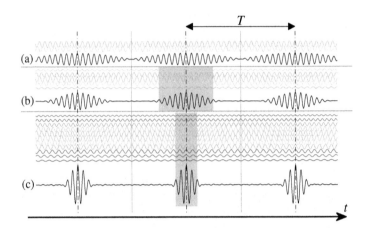

Figure 4.1:   Representation as a function of time t of the addition of 2 (a),
5 (b) and 11 (c) consecutive longitudinal modes. The black solid line shows the
total electric fields whereas the frequencies of individual longitudinal modes are
encoded in colors, from low frequencies (red) to high frequencies (blue).

Again, the number of oscillations produced by a longitudinal mode of frequency ν_n during a time t is equal to the product $\nu_n t$. One may conclude
that two modes separated by an amount called $\delta\nu$ will be shifted by half
an oscillation period after a time δt verifying the relation $\delta\nu\delta t = 1/2$. This
relation confirms what is illustrated in Figure 4.1: producing an ultra-
short pulse requires the addition of longitudinal modes spread over a broad
frequency range, $\delta\nu$, of the order of the inverse of the desired duration,
δt. Is a broad spectral range sufficient in itself to get short pulses? The
answer is clearly no, as can be easily deduced by considering the example
of sunlight. Despite an emission spectrum broader than the entire visible
spectrum, the sun is obviously not an ultrashort light source. In fact, for
longitudinal modes to add up into an ultrashort pulse, they need to be perfectly synchronized, which is indeed the case in Figure 4.1. The necessary
but not sufficient nature of the above condition translates into the general
inequality

$$\Delta\nu\Delta t \geq \frac{1}{4\pi},$$

where $\Delta\nu$ and Δt are respectively the spectral and temporal widths of
the pulse, as defined in terms of standard deviations. This relation, which
is the spectro-temporal analog of the Heisenberg inequality in quantum
physics, is extremely general and also holds in signal processing and in

acoustics. For example, the pitch of a percussion instrument such as the wood-block cannot be defined as accurately as that of a violin, due to the short duration of the sound in the first case, implying a broad frequency spectrum according to the above inequality.

To summarize this part on time and frequency, we note that the superposition of a large number of longitudinal modes results in a periodic pulse train, assuming these modes are properly synchronized. Let us remember, however, that we have assumed an empty cavity, so that we must now investigate how the presence of an amplifying medium might affect the shape of the pulse traveling back and forth inside the cavity.

4.3. Dispersion of a Femtosecond Pulse

Due to light–matter interaction, light cannot propagate as fast in a material medium as it would in vacuum. One defines the refractive index of a material as the ratio of the speed of light in vacuum by the speed of light propagating inside this material. Furthermore, since light–matter interaction is strongly dependent on the oscillation frequency of the electric field, so is the refractive index. As an example, this so-called dispersion of the refractive index is responsible for rainbows, which come from the color dependence of the angle of refraction through water droplets.

Due to the dispersion of the refractive index, and hence of the actual speed of light, different spectral components of an ultrashort pulse will not propagate at the same velocity in a material medium. In practice, it can be observed that — for visible radiation — smaller frequency components will propagate faster than greater frequency components: red is faster than blue. Let us now consider an ultrashort light pulse going through a material medium, such as a piece of glass or a transparent crystal, as shown in Figure 4.2. Different frequency components are encoded using the colors

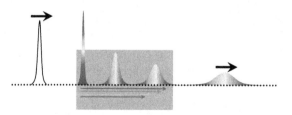

Figure 4.2: Broadening of an ultrashort pulse resulting from its propagation in matter. Due to the variation of the refractive index with frequency, the red part of the spectrum propagates faster than the blue part, resulting in a chirped pulse.

of the rainbow. We assume that for the incident pulse all frequency components are perfectly synchronized, which is sketched by stacking all colors
on top of one another for the pulse that just entered the medium. As the
pulse propagates through the medium, the faster red components get ahead
of the slower blue components, so that the transmitted pulse acquires the
shape illustrated in the figure. Red is now on the leading edge of the pulse
while blue is on the trailing edge. Such a pulse is said to be chirped, as the
continuous variation of frequency with time, when translated to a sound
wave, is reminiscent of the glissando found in some bird songs. The main
consequence of this chirp is that the transmitted pulse is longer than the
incident one. As an example, it can be calculated that a pulse with an initial duration of 10 fs would see its duration almost double after propagating
in a 1-mm thick Sapphire crystal. Considering the fact that crystals used
as amplifiers in femtosecond lasers are typically a few millimeter thick, it
is clear that this phenomenon must be taken care of. Otherwise, the light
pulse — assuming it could have been generated in the first place — would
spread out and completely vanish after only a few roundtrips inside the
cavity, which requires only a few tens of nanoseconds.

Optical physicists have developed a great variety of methods able to
compensate for the dispersion of ultrashort light pulses. Such methods
can be used either inside the cavity, in order to ensure a proper operation
of the laser, or outside the cavity, in order to finely tune the temporal
shape of the delivered pulses. Some of these latter devices, called pulse
shapers, can be quite elaborate and allow the programming of the exact
pulse shape, just like a function generator in electronics. However, inside
the laser cavity, one must favor simpler devices, less versatile but whose
low losses are compatible with an insertion inside a laser cavity.

Before concentrating on the so-called chirped mirror technique, let us
first discuss dielectric mirrors. A dielectric mirror is a periodic stack of
two different materials. Due to the difference in refractive index between
these two materials, a tiny fraction of the incident radiation is reflected at
each interface. Furthermore, if the layer thickness is chosen such that the
optical path difference between two consecutive reflections is a multiple of
the radiation wavelength, these tiny reflections will interfere constructively
and will eventually result in a global reflection coefficient close to 100%.
Such dielectric mirrors are widely used because of their ability to reflect
intense laser pulses with extremely low losses.

A chirped mirror, as shown in Figure 4.3, relies on the same principle
as a dielectric mirror except that the spatial period of alternation between

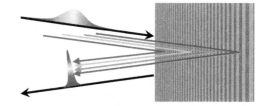

Figure 4.3: In a chirped mirror, the period of alternation between the two materials of different refractive indices varies with the depth inside the mirror, so that large (resp. small) wavelengths, reflected by the part of the mirror where the period is greater (resp. smaller), travel a greater (resp. smaller) distance.

the two materials now depends on the depth. Constructive interferences will thus occur at different depths according to the wavelength. As shown in the figure, the mirror is designed in such a way that the blue part of the spectrum is reflected by the part of the mirror that is closer to the surface, whereas the red part will need to propagate deeper inside the mirror before being reflected. The blue will then propagate over a shorter distance than the red, thereby compensating for the chirp of the initial pulse. Although the so-called negative dispersion of such an individual mirror remains limited, a large number of reflections will make chirp compensation practical.

4.4. Basic Principle of a Femtosecond Laser

Combining the different building blocks introduced above, we can now understand the general principle of operation of a femtosecond laser. We have seen that a short pulse duration Δt requires a large spectral width $\Delta \nu$, which requires a laser medium able to sustain amplification over a broad bandwidth. One of the best materials suitable for this purpose is Sapphire doped with Titanium ions, or Titanium:Sapphire (see Figure 2.3), which is capable of amplifying wavelength components between 650 and 1100 nm. Population inversion is ensured by pumping with a continuous-wave laser, typically a solid-state frequency-doubled diode-pumped laser. Finally, in order to avoid pulse broadening inside the laser cavity, the positive dispersion resulting from propagation through the laser amplifier must be compensated for by the negative dispersion resulting from bouncing off chirped mirrors. These simple principles result in the cavity design shown in Figure 4.4.

Let us follow the propagation of an ultrashort pulse inside the cavity, starting when the pulse enters the Titanium:Sapphire crystal (a). Thanks

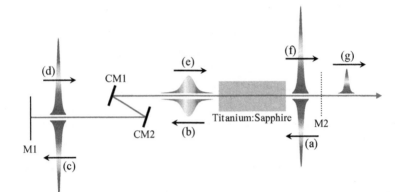

Figure 4.4:   Propagation of a femtosecond pulse inside the laser cavity, consisting of a Titanium:Sapphire crystal, a 100% reflecting mirror (M1), a partially-reflecting mirror (M2) allowing for a small fraction of the energy to be transmitted outside the cavity, and two chirped mirrors (CM1 and CM2). The pump laser is not shown.

to stimulated emission, the pulse will be slightly amplified upon propagation through the crystal, but it will also acquire some amount of chirp due to the positive dispersion of the crystal: the red is now ahead of the blue (b). This positive chirp will be compensated for upon reflections on chirped mirrors CM1 and CM2, so that all colors are now synchronized in the ultrashort pulse (c). The pulse reflected off mirror M1 (d) goes again through two reflections off chirped mirrors CM2 and CM1, so that red components will be further delayed as compared to blue components. The resulting pulse (e) exhibits a so-called negative chirp, which means that the blue is now ahead of the red. This is exactly the right amount of negative chirp for a perfect pre-compensation of the amplifying crystal positive dispersion, so that the amplified pulse (f) is now as short as possible. Note that pulse (f) is slightly more intense than pulse (a) thanks to amplification after a double pass through the Titanium:Sapphire crystal. This excess amount of energy makes possible the regeneration of pulse (a) — with the same energy and duration — while a small fraction of the pulse is transmitted through the partially-transmitting mirror M2, generating the output pulse (g) which constitutes the laser output beam.

    A femtosecond laser is therefore a device allowing us to concentrate all available energy into an ultrashort period of time. As compared to a continuous-wave laser of same average power, the peak power, i.e., the power at the peak of the pulse, will be enhanced by a huge factor, of the order of the number of longitudinal modes involved in the laser emission. This means a peak power about a million times greater than what would be available using a continuous-wave laser. At this level of power, the nonlinear optical processes mentioned in the introduction will come into play, which is the topic of the next section.

4.5. Nonlinear Optics and Kerr Effect

In order to understand nonlinear effects, it is useful to first briefly review the physical processes responsible for the optical index of refraction. As a first approximation, an atomic or molecular system can be modeled as a dipole: a positively-charged nucleus and a negatively-charged electron cloud. In the presence of an electromagnetic wave, the electron cloud is submitted to two forces: the restoring force associated with the Coulomb electrostatic attraction exerted by the nucleus and the Lorentz force induced by the electromagnetic wave. At the atomic level, the electric field of the wave can be described as a highly uniform field oscillating at high frequency. The motion of the electron cloud is then reduced to that of a forced harmonic oscillator, so that the electron cloud oscillates around the nucleus at the optical frequency with an amplitude which is proportional to the amplitude of the electromagnetic wave. This oscillating dipole radiates a delayed electromagnetic field which interferes with the exciting field. The final outcome is that, at a macroscopic scale, the light velocity in the considered medium is slower than in vacuum, and thus takes the form of the speed of light in vacuum divided by a number greater than 1, which is the refractive index. A key result is that as long as the dipole behaves as a harmonic oscillator, the index of refraction does not depend on the light intensity.

However, under intense illumination, the oscillation amplitude of the electron cloud might become so large that the attractive force between the core and the electron cloud is no longer proportional to the displacement, so that the system no longer behaves as a harmonic oscillator. The response of the oscillator then depends on the light intensity and may produce new optical frequencies such as the harmonics of the fundamental frequency: double frequency, triple, etc.

Among the great variety of nonlinear optical processes, the optical Kerr effect, also known as quadratic electro-optic effect, is a change in the refractive index of a material in response to the optical intensity I. As a first approximation, the optical index scales linearly with the intensity, so that

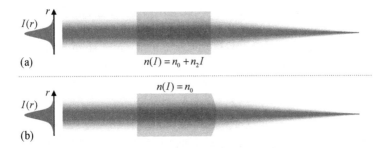

Figure 4.5: (a) Propagation of a Gaussian laser beam in a Kerr medium. The optical intensity being greater at the center of the beam, the effective index of refraction is increased by the Kerr effect. The resulting greater optical path at the center of the beam is equivalent to (b) which corresponds to a linear medium with a convex interface, which is nothing but a lens.

the intensity-dependent refractive index can be written as

$$n(I) = n_0 + n_2 I,$$

where n_0 is the refractive index of the medium and n_2 is the nonlinear index of refraction, of positive sign in most cases. The optical Kerr effect bears consequences in time as well as in space domain, both of these aspects playing a key role in femtosecond lasers.

The spatial manifestation of the Kerr effect is illustrated in Figure 4.5. The index of refraction — hence the optical path length as well — is increased at the center of the beam where the intensity is greater, which induces an effective lens in the medium. In turn, this lens, called the Kerr lens, tends to focus the transmitted beam. This phenomenon is called self-focusing since the Kerr lens is induced by the beam itself, or more precisely through the interaction of the beam with the nonlinear medium.

The time-domain manifestation of the optical Kerr effect is more difficult to grasp, although there is a deep mathematical connection between the time- and space-domain effects. Consider a short pulse propagating through a nonlinear non-dispersive medium as shown in Figure 4.6. Under the combined effects of the Kerr effect and of the time-dependent intensity of the exciting pulse, the refractive index now varies over time. It increases during the rising edge of the pulse, while it decreases during the trailing edge. Let us first consider what happens during the rising edge. The light then propagates in a medium in which the optical thickness — which is the product of the thickness of the medium by the refractive index — grows over time. This is exactly as if the radiation source were moving away from

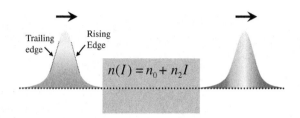

Figure 4.6: Propagation of an ultrashort pulse in a Kerr medium, resulting in the generation of new frequencies.

the observer. Due to the Doppler effect, there will be a down-shift of the observed frequency, in much the same way as when a fast car with a noisy motor or siren moves away from you. In contrast, when the car is moving in your direction, the Doppler effect prescribes an increase in the perceived sound frequency — hence the clear decrease in pitch when the car just went your height. Similarly, during the falling edge of the optical pulse, the refractive index decreases over time, which implies that the optical path decreases. The source is now approaching the observer and the Doppler effect results in a shift towards higher frequencies.

It follows that the optical Kerr effect produces a pulse containing new frequencies as compared to those constituting the incident pulse. As in the case of dispersion, the generated pulse exhibits a positive chirp, since the leading edge is red-shifted while the trailing edge is blue-shifted. However, it is important to note the difference between these two phenomena. In the case of dispersion, the spectral components are already present in the incident pulse and are shifted in time which results in a lengthening of the pulse. Conversely, in the case of the optical Kerr effect, the pulse duration does not change while new frequencies, which were not necessarily present in the initial pulse, are created.

The optical Kerr effect, coupled to other nonlinear effects which are beyond the scope of this book, gives rise to a spectacular phenomenon that can be easily observed with a femtosecond laser: continuum generation. In fact, the production of new frequencies is so efficient that a pure white light can be generated, as observed in Figure 4.7.

4.6. Mode-Locking

After this brief detour through nonlinear optics, it is now possible to better understand the real physics involved in femtosecond lasers. So far, two

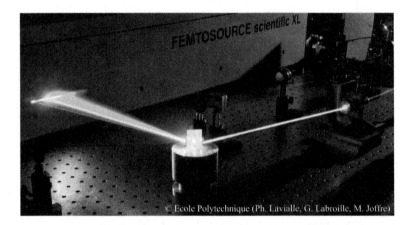

Figure 4.7: The beam of a femtosecond laser (Femtosource scientific XL 500, Femtolasers, Austria) is focused (on the right of the picture) in a transparent medium. Considering the pulse energy (500 nJ) and duration (50 fs), the nonlinear interaction in the medium results in the generation of a much broader spectrum. The different spectral components of this *white laser beam* are spread by a prism.

crucial points have been ignored. First, there is no requirement for the laser represented in Figure 4.4 to actually operate in pulsed mode, so that we lack a selection mechanism. Second, it is important to note that the closing relationship is more difficult to fulfill in a femtosecond laser than for a single-mode laser. Indeed, the *whole* pulse must be perfectly reproduced, identical to itself, after each roundtrip in the cavity, which is far more demanding than reproducing the same amplitude and phase of a single-mode laser. Addressing these two issues is the purpose of mode-locking, a process that provides a stable synchronization of longitudinal modes. In most femtosecond lasers using a Titanium:Sapphire crystal, the mode-locking process is achieved by the optical Kerr effect in the laser crystal itself. There are of course other means for achieving mode-locking, such as the use of a saturable absorber as described in Figure 2.10 of Chapter 2. The optical Kerr effect described in this chapter, which is totally negligible in steady-state operation (low power), will instead modify the spatial profile of the beam in pulsed mode (high power) through the process of self-focusing illustrated in Figure 4.5. Femtosecond oscillators are thus deliberately designed so that losses in steady-state regime are higher than in pulsed regime. For example, a patented technique consists in placing a slit at a suitable location in the cavity. Like any good laser, the oscillator will seek for minimized losses, which favors the pulsed regime since the beam sneaks easier through the slit inside the cavity.

The second issue highlighted above is related to the closing condition: the dispersion of the cavity must be perfectly canceled so that the temporal shape of the pulse can be identically reproduced after one roundtrip. It is simply impossible to do so by using only dispersive mirrors because the compensation cannot be completely accurate over the entire laser spectrum. Any residual deformation, even small, would accumulate after many roundtrips in the cavity and would eventually destroy the pulse, if it could ever form. In fact, instead of trying to compensate exactly the intracavity dispersion, dispersive mirrors can be used to intentionally overcompensate the overall dispersion of the cavity: mirrors with larger dispersion can be selected or the number of reflections can be increased. The idea is that the negative dispersion provided by the dispersive mirrors should be greater (in absolute terms) than the positive dispersion induced by the linear propagation in the laser crystal. Thus, the net dispersion of the cavity will be negative. Consider again Figure 4.4 and particularly pulse (e) which has a negative chirp. We now know that this chirp is *too* strong. The pulse transmitted by the crystal (f) would have a residual negative chirp without the optical Kerr effect. The latter, due to the process shown in Figure 4.6, will produce a red shift of the leading edge of the pulse and a blue shift of the trailing edge, which will cancel the residual chirp to produce the shortest possible pulse at the output of the crystal, and thus of the laser. Since the optical Kerr effect depends on the exact shape of the pulse, we have now the adjustable parameter we lacked earlier to ensure a perfect compensation of the dispersion of the cavity. In its constant struggle to ensure emission, the laser is continuously adjusting the exact shape of the pulse to exactly fulfill the closing condition.

Mode-locking has an essential impact on the position of the longitudinal modes. In Section 4.2, we saw that the modes were equidistant and spaced by $1/T$, but in principle this was only theoretical idealization, resulting from the assumption of an empty cavity. In practice, the period T of the cavity depends on the frequency ν of the considered mode because of the residual cavity dispersion. In the case of a negative residual dispersion, the period T decreases with frequency since bluest components propagate faster than the reddest. The spacing between the longitudinal modes is therefore expected to increase with frequency. However, thanks to the balance between the optical Kerr effect and the residual negative dispersion of the cavity, for a specific shape of the pulse produced, all the spectral components share

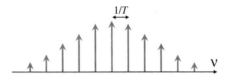

Figure 4.8: Frequency comb of a femtosecond laser. A real spectrum contains
up to several millions of perfectly equidistant modes.

exactly the same propagation time in the cavity. This creates a perfectly
uniform frequency comb, as shown in Figure 4.8. By stabilizing the period T
of the cavity to an atomic clock, physicists were able to show that the
relative accuracy of a frequency comb could reach 10^{-17}. Such a precision
has revolutionized the field of frequency metrology, as will be discussed in
the next chapter.

4.7. Amplification

The typical peak power produced by a femtosecond oscillator, although
moderate, is already sufficient to induce interesting nonlinear effects in
materials. The best example is probably the optical Kerr effect discussed
above which is central in mode-locking femtosecond oscillators. Nevertheless, it often takes more energy for an effective use of these nonlinear effects.
At the output of a femtosecond oscillator, pulses have a typical energy which
ranges from a fraction of a nanojoule ($1\,\mathrm{nJ} = 10^{-9}\,\mathrm{J}$) to a few hundred nano-
joules. To increase the energy per pulse, the pulses need to be amplified
by consecutive laser amplifiers. It is however not so straightforward to do
so with ultrashort pulses. Indeed, even with large-area optical beams, the
damage threshold level of the amplifying media is quickly reached.

To increase the pulse energy to the millijoule, Joule or the kilojoule
level, it is necessary to use a technique called *chirped pulse amplification*.
This technique, inspired by previous works on radars, consists in reducing
the peak power in the amplification stages by deliberately increasing the
pulse duration. The amplification is obtained in three stages: the pulses are
temporally stretched, amplified and then recompressed (see Figure 2.12 of
Chapter 2). The amplification mechanism is based on stimulated emission
as explained in Chapter 1. However, as the laser gain varies with wavelength, some wavelengths are more amplified than others, which tends to
reduce the spectral width. In a femtosecond oscillator, the effect of spectral
gain narrowing is exactly compensated by the spectral broadening induced

by the optical Kerr effect. In an amplifier, spectral gain narrowing leads to a dilemma: as the energy is increased, the amplified spectrum gets narrower and the recompressed pulses get longer. In practice, it is difficult to amplify pulses of less than 20 fs at energy levels much above the millijoule. Nevertheless, it is possible to reach energies of several hundred Joules and corresponding powers that are measured today in petawatts (10^{15} W). The electric fields of these giant lasers will, in the near future, accelerate charged particles at relativistic speeds comparable to those of particle accelerators.

4.8. Generation of Attosecond Pulses

One of the most disputed frontiers in the area of ultrashort pulse synthesis is naturally the shortest duration achievable. The record duration has long been limited to a barrier of a few femtoseconds, which is both related to the period of oscillation of the electric field and to the width of the spectrum available in the visible spectral range. A nonlinear phenomenon discovered in the late 1980s, high order harmonics generation (HHG), allowed breaking this femtosecond limit in the early 2000's.

HHG is based on the tunnel effect that arises in an atom submitted to a strong oscillating electric field. Let us get back temporarily to the model of the elastically bound electron depicted in Section 4.5 but now using electrostatic potentials to formulate it: the electron is trapped in a potential well created by the positive charge of the nucleus, with a negative energy level. When this model atom experiences the extremely intense electric field of an ultrashort laser, an electric potential is added to the one of the ionic core. The surface potential corresponding to this field is a plane whose slope varies with the absolute value and the sign of the electric field. The sum of the atomic potential and of the potential associated with the light field takes a complicated form (Figure 4.9). If the electric field of the laser is sufficiently intense, the total potential is lowered below the energy of the electron which then freely leaves the potential well (field-ionization). For slightly less intense a field, the electron should remain bound. However, it has a nonzero chance to cross over this barrier by a purely quantum effect called tunneling. Indeed, at this level of description, the electron must also be considered as a wave whose behavior departs from that of a classical particle. In a quantum view, part of the electron wave gets outside the well, while another part stays inside. The key point is that the *amount* of wave which gets outside the well varies very rapidly with the residual height of the barrier. In practice, the electron can escape the well only when

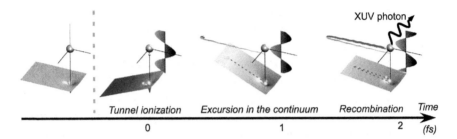

Figure 4.9: Three-step model of HHG. (a) Isolated atom and associated electrostatic potential. (b) Submitted to an intense electric field represented in gray,
an electron gets out of the potential through tunneling. (c–d) The electric field
evolves, first tearing off the electron from the origin and then bringing it back,
transferring energy to it. Finally, this energy gets restituted in (d) through XUV
radiation.

the gate is lowered to a minimum, that is to say when the electric field of
light is extremum. This *time window* is obviously extremely narrow, even
compared to the period of the laser field. Then time passes and the laser
field follows its quasi-periodic evolution: during half a cycle of its period,
the laser field vanishes gradually, and then becomes negative. The electron
which has left the well, accelerates, then decelerates accordingly to finally
turn back (about 1 fs in Figure 4.9). It then speeds up again in the opposite
direction gaining a lot of energy and, under certain conditions, returns to
the vicinity of its parent nucleus about 2/3 of the laser period later. It
interacts with it and a possible outcome of this interaction is the emission,
as an electromagnetic radiation, of the energy that it has gained during its
tour away from the nucleus. Actually, the more intense the field, the more
energy the electron may gain. Photons having up to 300 times the energy of
the pump photon have been observed. The frequency of the photon being
proportional to its energy, the emission is in the XUV spectral range.

The process is controlled by the pump laser: an electron which would
come out of the ionic potential slightly earlier than another is driven by
an electric field with a slightly different shape, acquiring a different energy
and having a different return time. So the emitted photons have neither all
the same energy nor all the same emission time. The result is a very broad
but imperfectly synchronized spectrum in the XUV range. It is possible
to compensate for this time drift of the energy components by inserting
appropriate dispersive materials in the XUV beam, eventually forming an
attosecond pulse.

There is little doubt that attosecond pulses were generated this way in the 1990s. However, devices adapted to the measurement of such short durations had not yet been invented and evidence of attosecond structure was finally given only in 2001. The technique is as follows. An attosecond pulse is focused in an atomic gas in the presence of a synchronized "dressing" infrared laser field, which has a very long duration in comparison with the XUV one. The energy of the XUV photons being greater than the ionization energy of the atoms, they get ionized and the electrons take away (in the form of kinetic energy) the energy difference between the XUV photons and the height of the barrier. The simultaneous presence of the infrared field subsequently alters the energy that the electrons take away, which finally also depends on the value of the IR field at the very time of ionization. Thus, if all XUV photons were synchronous, the corresponding additional energies of the electrons would all be identical. Conversely, if they are not synchronous, electrons take away different energies. By scanning the delay between the attosecond pulse and the dressing pulse, the energy of the electrons is then modulated and the analysis of this modulation provides a measurement of the relative timing of the XUV spectral components. This is known as the Rabbit or FROG-CRAB technique. Two examples of its use are shown in Figure 4.10. In the first case, the infrared laser was extremely short, less than 3 fs. At one given delay (a given abscissa), a continuous electron spectrum is obtained. The position in energy of this spectrum is modulated by the infrared beam. In addition to the measurement of the attosecond pulse, the figure also shows an image of the infrared electric field used for the dressing, which is encoded in the electronic spectrum. In the second example, the generating laser is longer, about 35 fs, i.e., about 10 periods of the laser field at half maximum. The figure represents three periods. At a given delay, the spectrum is now modulated: plotted versus the energy, a section shows a series of peaks located at odd multiples of the photon energy of the generating laser. These peaks occur because the pump laser is sufficiently long to lower several times the potential barrier of the atoms in the generation gas. A series of attosecond pulses is thus obtained, whose temporal separation is half a cycle of the generating field. In the spectral domain, this periodicity in time results in a comb of frequencies, like the longitudinal modes of a femtosecond laser results from the periodicity of the pulse train. The phenomenon was discovered in this kind of configuration, hence its name *high order harmonic generation*. In terms of measurement, the same kind of pattern as in the case of an isolated pulse is obtained: the spectrum shows a periodic modulation following the delay

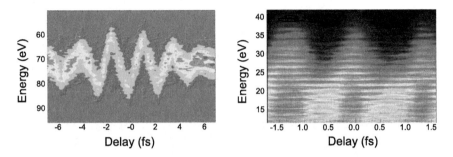

Figure 4.10:   Attosecond pulses/IR cross correlation traces in the case of a single attosecond pulse (left) and a train (right). In ordinate are shown the energies of the radiation and the abscissa axis is the time delay between the two fields. [From M. Schultze *et al.*, *New J. Phys.* **9**, 243 (2007) and P. Johnsson *et al.*, *Phys. Rev. Lett.* **95**, 013001 (2005). Copyright (2007) Institute of Physics and (2005) American Physical Society.]

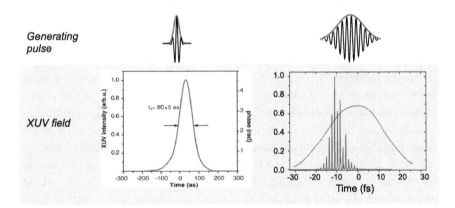

Figure 4.11:   Temporal profiles of attosecond pulses reconstructed from traces similar to those displayed in Figure 4.10 when (left) a short pump pulse (single attosecond pulse), and (right) a long pump pulse (train of attosecond pulses) is used. [From E. Goulielmakis *et al.*, *Science* **320**, 1614 (2008) and V. Tosa *et al.*, *Phys. Rev. A* **79**, 043828 (2009). Copyright (2008) American Association for the Advancement of Science and (2009) American Physical Society.]

between the generating laser field and the attosecond pulse. The temporal forms reported in Figure 4.11 are derived from the use of a reconstruction algorithm on traces similar to those of Figure 4.10. The first is one of the shortest pulses measured to date which is ≃80 as long. This corresponds to a width of ≃30 eV. The second reconstruction shows a pulse train of 150 as duration as an average, under part of the envelope of the generating laser field reported as a dashed line.

This new source paves the way for innovative applications. A key feature, besides its duration, is that it inherits the main properties of the generating laser, and in particular its coherence. The experiment described above, firstly used for the characterization of attosecond pulses through their interaction with a known species in presence of an infrared femtosecond pulse, is quite often also used for applications: instead of a species with well known photoionization properties, an unknown species is injected in the detector and shone with attosecond pulses characterized beforehand. It should be noted that this technology is new but growing fast. Obtaining such pulses remains difficult: about twenty laboratories around the world have observed them to date. It appears to be limited to pulses of the order of a few tens of attoseconds at best, on the one hand because of the width of the spectrum generated and secondly because of the difficulty to finely time the components of the emitted spectrum. Other avenues are being explored. We can, in particular, mention the generation of harmonics on solid targets. However, to date, the harmonic sources in gases are the shortest ever light sources, they are well characterized, and open new perspectives. For example, the first steps have been recently overcome to eventually follow, through a series of images of electronic clouds, the first moments of a chemical reaction, realizing a molecular tomography.

Chapter 5

Ultrastable Lasers and High-Precision Measurements

Christian Chardonnet

CNRS Senior Researcher,
Laboratoire de Physique des Lasers, Université Paris 13,
Villetaneuse, France

Pierre-François Cohadon

Associate Professor,
Ecole Normale Supérieure, Laboratoire Kastler Brossel,
Paris, France

Saïda Guellati-Khélifa

Professor, Conservatoire National des Arts et Métiers,
Laboratoire Kastler Brossel,
Paris, France

Lasers quickly escaped research laboratories to be included in just a few years' time into a large number of everyday life applications, but they remain a yet unrivaled tool for fundamental physics. This chapter presents the main characteristics of the lasers that physicists take advantage of in precision measurements, and a few examples of such measurements.

A laser beam is characterized by a number of features: wavelength (or frequency), amplitude (or intensity), but also phase, position (in the plane of a detector for instance), propagation direction, or even polarization state. All these features can be measured even if, in practice, the experimental setup has to transform them into an intensity, the only property directly measurable with a photodetector.

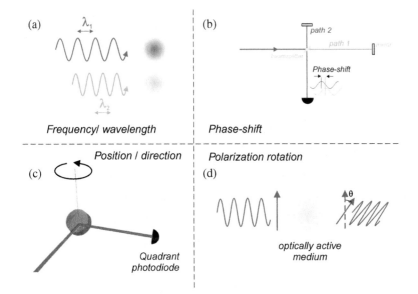

Figure 5.1: Main characteristics one can measure on a laser beam, and associated physics experiments. (a) The resonance wavelength of light can be used to identify an atomic or molecular species. (b) The phase-shift between two paths allows to measure their length difference. (c) The position or direction of a beam can be used to probe a mirror rotation. (d) The polarization rotation of a beam yields informations on the medium it went through.

Figure 5.1 presents examples of such experimental setups. A *spectroscopy* experiment consists in acquiring the list of the frequencies of the light either absorbed or emitted by a medium. This can be used either to characterize the medium (if one knows its composition, ideally a single atom or molecular species), or to identify it (using a spectroscopic atlas, which is a long list of resonance frequencies of one or a number of species of atoms or molecules). An *interferometry* experiment converts a phase shift between two different optical paths into an intensity change; such an experiment allows one to measure very small displacements. A mirror rotation can be measured as well with a reflected laser beam, via its position on a position-sensitive detector such as a quadrant photodiode. Finally, one can characterize a medium (either crystalline or of biological interest) by the way the polarization state of light changes along the propagation in the medium.

In the following, we will primarily focus on frequency and phase-shifts measurements.

5.1.   An Ultrastable Light Source

The key instrument for all these measurements is a laser, quite often a *single-mode* laser, characterized by a single emission frequency. In many experiments indeed, the simultaneous presence of different laser frequencies would scramble the experimental signal and therefore has to be avoided. We have already seen in Chapter 1 how the possible emission wavelength of a laser depends on the cavity length. We have seen as well that quite often, the gain curve of the amplifying medium is broad enough to accommodate multiple laser lines.

5.1.1.   *How to make a laser single mode?*

Figure 5.2 explains the technique used to make a laser oscillate in a single mode: embed in the laser cavity an optical filter, e.g., an additional cavity. As this cavity is much shorter than the main laser cavity, its free spectral range $c/2L$ is much larger and can be of the same order of magnitude as the width of the gain curve. The combined effect of both filtering effects — by setting both cavities at resonance simultaneously for a given frequency — therefore allows us to pinpoint a single longitudinal mode of the laser: laser emission then occurs at one and only one wavelength.

5.1.2.   *How to reduce the spectral width of a laser?*

But having a laser oscillate with a single wavelength (or a single frequency) may be insufficient: this frequency may still fluctuate or drift over time,

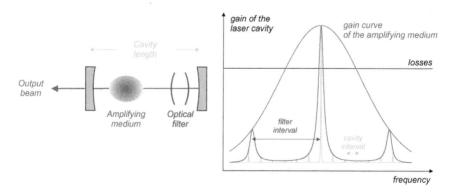

Figure 5.2:   How to make a single-mode laser. The laser emission range is limited to a single very narrow peak by combining the cavity filtering effect (strong, but with plenty of possible resonance peaks) with the one of an additional optical filter (not so strong, but with just one possible frequency).

following the cavity length changes, which may be detrimental to some experiments.

As an example, we have already seen that the energy efficiency of some lasers can be pretty low: most of the power used to pump the active medium is actually wasted into heat. A water cooling system (with cold water used to release some heat out of the active medium) is sometimes used to avoid excessive heating (and damage) of the material. Such a system has the drawback of inducing vibrations that may shift the cavity length. Averaged over a fraction of a second, the whole set of *instantaneous laser emission frequencies* can be considered as one central frequency blurred by an uncertainty, the *spectral width* of the laser. The same heating process may also cause the cavity to steadily expand, resulting in a drift of the laser emission frequency.

Figure 5.3 explains the principle of a *frequency locking* of the laser. Such a locking consists in picking off a part of the beam at the cavity output and using it to compare the laser frequency with a reference frequency. Depending on the experiment performed, the reference can be absolute, using an atomic or a molecular resonance whose frequency is known accurately under given experimental conditions, or relative, for example a cavity insulated from external disturbance, whose resonance frequencies are extremely stable, even if their absolute values are unknown. This signal is then used to perform a feedback on the cavity length. The correction to apply usually

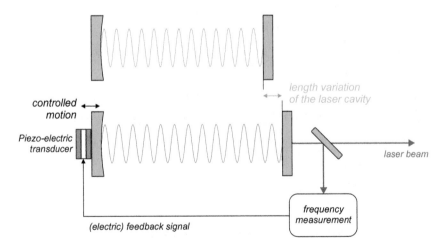

Figure 5.3: Connection between cavity length fluctuations and the emitted wavelength, and principle of a laser locking scheme.

is a fraction of the wavelength, thereby allowing the use of piezoelectric transducers to move one of the mirrors and adjust the cavity length. If, at any time, a vibration slightly stretches the cavity, the frequency measurement setup monitors a decrease of the emission frequency and the *feedback loop* proceeds to compensate for it. As the frequency gets closer to the target value, the feedback signal decreases and eventually vanishes when the desired value is reached. Inversely when the cavity is shortened. One of the issues that the experimental physicist faces is to implement a feedback loop fast enough to efficiently counteract external disturbances.

We focused here on the stabilization of the frequency of a single-mode laser, but similar techniques can be used to limit the fluctuations of other laser features such as intensity, beam shape... One can thereby obtain at will a laser beam close to an ideal laser beam.

5.2. Laser Spectroscopy

Absorption spectroscopy consists in continuously tuning the wavelength of a light source which interacts with a material medium and to detect the transmitted intensity. The obtained signal is called a spectrum. For some very precise wavelengths, light can be at resonance with the medium. This light is partially or totally absorbed. By detecting the intensity of the transmitted light through the medium which modulates the absorption, we have access to its characteristic frequencies.

5.2.1. *The laser: an ideal source for spectroscopy*

The art of spectroscopy from the origin was to develop methods which allow one to reduce as much as possible the width of the individual resonances. The interest is twofold: the width of the resonances characterizes the resolution of the spectroscopic method and thus determines the minimum distance between two resonance frequencies of the medium which can be distinguished. The great advance of the laser has been to provide a light source whose spectrum is so narrow (see Figure 5.4) that in most cases, it does not broaden the detected resonance. The medium itself is responsible for the whole width of the resonances. Figure 5.5 shows the progress of resolution on a vibrational band of the SF_6 molecule. Before the laser era, the grid spectrometer revealed only the envelope of the band. The first spectra obtained with laser diodes had a resolution limited by the Doppler effect: the speed of the molecules shifts the resonance by $\vec{k} \cdot \vec{v}$ where $\vec{k}$ is the wave vector of the laser and $\vec{v}$ the molecular speed. The width of the resonance

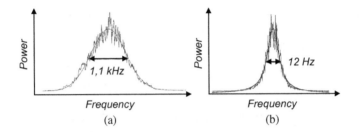

(a)   (b)

Figure 5.4:   Spectrum of a CO_2 laser. Laser frequency: 30 THz. The electric field emitted by the laser does not vary in time as a perfect sine wave because of a number of noises. Its energy is slightly distributed around its central frequency. (a) Spectral linewidth of the free-running laser: 1.1 kHz (b) After locking, the laser linewidth is divided by 100.

is then ku where u is the mean quadratic velocity of the molecules in the gas, which is related to its temperature. The linewidth is of the order of a few tens of MHz up to GHz depending on the wavelength of the laser.

To go beyond this limit, sub-Doppler spectroscopy methods were developed, especially saturated absorption: a standing wave is formed with two counterpropagating traveling waves. There exists a simple resonance condition with the two waves: $\omega - \vec{k} \cdot \vec{v} = \omega_0$ and $\omega + \vec{k} \cdot \vec{v} = \omega_0$, where ω is the laser angular frequency and ω_0 is the molecule resonance frequency. This condition is fulfilled only for molecules such that $\vec{v}$ and $\vec{k}$ are perpendicular. This generates a signal with a so-called *homogeneous* width much smaller than the Doppler width. Figure 5.5(c) is obtained with a free-running laser, Figure 5.5(d) with a frequency-controlled laser. A linewidth of 1 kHz is obtained, which corresponds to a 30,000-fold reduction compared to the Doppler width. The hyperfine structure due to the magnetic dipoles of the nuclei is observed and perfectly matches the theoretical value.

The spectroscopic methods are the finest methods that we can imagine to analyze matter. As an example, they are also used in the physics of atmosphere for the detection of traces or of pollutants.

5.2.2.   *The calibration issue*

Spectroscopy requires calibrating the frequency axis of the spectra. Figure 5.5(b) reveals the vibration-rotation structure of the SF_6 molecule. In order to analyze the structure, the distance between resonances must be measured, but also the so-called *absolute frequency* of the resonance. This requires measuring the laser frequency, which turns out to be a very complex

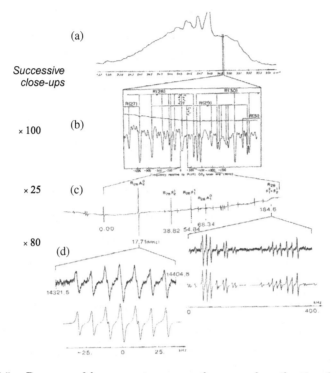

Figure 5.5: Progress of laser spectroscopy: the case of a vibrational band of the SF_6 molecule. (a) 1970: Before the laser era, spectrum obtained with a grid spectrometer; (b) 1973: Absorption spectroscopy with a laser diode; (c) 1977: Saturated absorption spectroscopy with a free-running CO_2 laser (d) 1983 identical to (c), but with a frequency-stabilized laser. (From C. J. Bordé, Revue du Cethedec, Ondes et Signal NS83-1 (1983).

question. Let us remind that the primary frequency standard is given by a hyperfine transition of the cesium atom at approximately 9.2 GHz, while the laser frequencies are from 1,000 up to 100,000 times higher, between the far infrared and the ultraviolet spectrum. Until 10 years ago, starting from a cesium clock, one had to set up a frequency multiplication chain of incredible complexity. It required exotic intermediate lasers to finally measure one or a few atomic or molecular frequencies in a specific spectral band. These absolute frequencies so painfully measured served as secondary frequency standards to calibrate spectra in their immediate vicinity. Then the most precise way to calibrate a spectrum consists in locking the laser frequency on the top of an atomic or molecular resonance of known frequency. It is easily understood that the narrower the resonance, the higher the precision one can achieve on the position of the resonance peak. An accuracy equivalent to 1/1000 of the linewidth is easily obtained. The very high resolution spectroscopy methods are thus used for the best frequency control.

Then the beat note between a locked laser and a laser of nearby frequency can be detected by a fast photodetector if the difference is in the radio-frequency domain. By acting on the frequency of the second laser, one can lock the beat frequency on a very stable radio-frequency. A continuous tuning of this radio-frequency will induce a variation of the laser frequency in a perfectly controlled and known way, well suited for very high resolution spectroscopy and spectra calibration. The spectra of Figure 5.5(d) have been recorded with this method and one can notice that theory accounts very well even for the details of the hyperfine structure.

5.3.　Recent Progress

5.3.1.　The frequency-comb revolution

Time and frequency metrology has experienced a huge revolution at the end of the 1990s thanks to the use of femtosecond lasers to connect frequencies issued from very different spectral regions.

What is the principle? In Chapter 4, we learned that a femtosecond laser is a mode-locked laser which emits a pulse train. The time T between two pulses is the time for a roundtrip of the light in the cavity. The inverse of T, called f_{rep} is the frequency difference between two successive modes. Figure 5.6 shows that the laser spectrum (in red) is composed of a comb of equidistant frequencies. It has been shown that the modes are perfectly equidistant within better than one part in 10^{18}. f_{rep} depends on the cavity length and is generally between 100 MHz and 1 GHz, i.e., in the radio-frequency domain. For a typical femtosecond laser, as the Titanium–Sapphire laser which typically delivers pulses of 25 fs, the total width of the spectrum is 40 THz in the near infrared (wavelength near 850 nm). The number of modes in the spectrum is thus between 40,000 and 400,000, all of them perfectly equally spaced. We thus obtain a frequency comb of very numerous teeth that we can use as a ruler to very precisely measure the unknown laser frequency.

The principle is to detect the beat note between the laser to be measured and the femtosecond laser and to measure the beat frequency between the unknown frequency and the closest mode of the femtosecond laser. Note that the identification of the order n of this closest mode already requires an

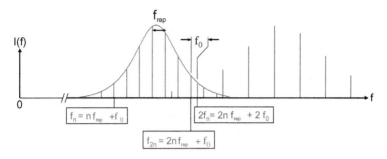

Figure 5.6: Frequency comb of a femtosecond laser used in metrology. The laser spectrum is plotted in red. The modes f_n of the laser are spaced with a constant splitting, f_{rep}. The comb of the frequency doubled laser is plotted in blue. The comparison of the two combs allows one to measure the offset, f_0 (self-referencing technique). After calibration, the red frequency comb can be used to measure any unknown laser frequency in the vicinity of the comb frequencies.

approximate knowledge of the laser frequency to be measured. This beat note frequency is smaller than f_{rep} and thus falls in the radio-frequency domain, which can be in the detection bandwidth of the photodetectors. However, a difficulty occurs here: the comb frequencies are not exactly equal to nf_{rep} but are shifted by an offset frequency f_0 which can be chosen below f_{rep}: $f_n = nf_{\text{rep}} + f_0$. f_0 is a quantity which varies with the laser intensity, a mechanism that we will not explain here.

However, the value of f_0 is required for the frequency measurement. For that purpose, a *self-referencing* method has been developed and is illustrated on Figure 5.6. A first step consists in considerably broadening the spectrum of the frequency comb typically from 40 THz up to 300 THz. In that case the comb covers more than one octave with extreme frequencies of 200 and 500 THz. The comb frequencies are still of the general form $f_n = nf_{\text{rep}} + f_0$. Such a stretching may be performed by sending the laser beam into a photonic-crystal fiber of a few cm long. These new fibers with exceptional properties were introduced at the end of the 1990s and revolutionized the field of nonlinear optics. The second step consists in extracting a fraction of the stretched comb in order to feed a nonlinear crystal acting as a frequency doubler. It generates a second comb of frequencies $2 \times (nf_{\text{rep}} + f_0)$. The beat frequency between the nth mode of the doubled comb and the $2n$th mode of the original stretched comb is exactly f_0, which can be measured. The optical frequency of any tooth of the comb can thus be determined by measuring f_{rep} and f_0 relative to the reference frequency provided by a clock based on a cesium fountain (the principle of which will be presented in the next chapter). We are now able to compare the frequency of a monomode laser to the very well-known frequency of one of the teeth of the comb of the femtosecond laser. The precision is not limited by the frequency comb but is usually limited by the laser source to be measured itself.

The clocks operating in the optical domain are on the way to outperform the cesium fountain, which operates in the microwave domain. With the help of the frequency comb, it will be possible to generate radio-frequencies with the same accuracy as optical frequencies. The discovery of the frequency comb and its use in metrology is the results of researches performed in Munich and at JILA (Boulder, Colorado). Their authors T. Hänsch and J.L. Hall obtained the Nobel Prize of Physics in 2005. Commercial devices are now on sale. The method is well suited for the optical domain as well as for the radio-frequency domain. The development of femtosecond lasers will soon allow us to use the same technique in the X-ray band. With laser cooling, the frequency combs revolutionized the field of frequency metrology. And their use is only at its very beginning.

5.3.2. *Cold atoms and optical clocks*

Cesium atomic clocks have reached impressive performance thanks to laser cooling of neutral atoms (see Section 2.4 of the next chapter). Nowadays, atomic clocks drift by only one second in 300 million years. Henceforth, frequency combs based on femtosecond lasers (described in the previous chapter) allow us to easily compare any two frequencies. But if the laser plays a crucial role for the performance of cesium clocks, the frequency of these clocks is not generated directly by a laser but by a microwave synthesizer.

In this section, we focus on the prospects to redefine the second using an atomic transition in the optical spectrum. In this case, the optical atomic clock should be realized using a laser whose frequency is stabilized on this atomic transition. Through the description of the most promising scheme to implement such atomic clock with neutral atoms, we hope to show the reader the scientific approach in metrology.

Let us begin by reminding the principle of an atomic clock. The method to measure time has always consisted in counting the periods of a cyclic phenomenon such as the rotation of the Earth, the swing of a mechanical pendulum, or the vibration of a quartz oscillator. The atomic clock is based

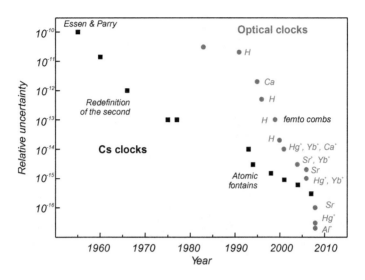

Figure 5.7: Evolution of the uncertainty of frequency measurements of atomic clocks for the last 60 years. Black squares represent Cs-based atomic clocks, red dots frequency measurements with an optical transition for a number of atoms and ions. The starting point *Essen & Parry* corresponds to the first atomic clock based on a Cs atomic beam, in 1955.

on the same principle: it consists in counting the vibrations of the electromagnetic wave absorbed during the atomic transition. Thus in 1967, at its 13th meeting, the General Conference on Weights and Measures defined the unit of time, the second, as follows: "The second is the duration of 9, 192, 631, 770 periods of the radiation corresponding to the transition between the two hyperfine levels of the ground state of the cesium 133 atom".

The interest in redefining the second using an atomic transition in the visible spectrum lies in the fact that the frequency of the visible light is tens of thousands of times higher than that of a microwave. Thus, if an atom is interrogated during a given time by an optical wave (provided by a laser for instance), it will be sensitive to tens of thousands of times as many oscillations of the laser field as if it was a microwave field, and this allows *a priori* a much more precise measurement of time.

Many obstacles have hindered for a long time the feasibility of optical clocks. The main difficulty comes from the absence of electronic systems fast enough to measure optical frequencies. We saw how the advent of the frequency combs at the end of the 1990s upset the landscape: the comparison of the radio-frequencies and the optical frequencies almost became

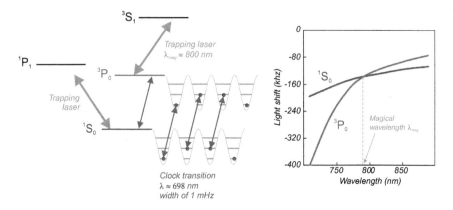

Figure 5.8: Left: Energy levels of the [88]Sr atom, used for an optical clock with an optical lattice. Right: Variations of the light-shifts of the energy levels $^1S_0$ and $^3P_0$ with respect to the wavelength.

easy as pie. Let us describe the principle of an optical clock using strontium atoms trapped in an optical lattice generated by standing laser waves (Figure 5.8). The trapping of atoms in these standing waves relies on the methods of laser cooling presented in the next chapter. The isotope 87 of strontium possesses all the virtues required to be used for an optical clock. We shall discuss this point later.

The principle, illustrated on Figure 5.9, consists in shining strontium atoms with a laser beam. The laser frequency is swept to probe the suitable atomic transition. A photodetector provides a response corresponding to the absorption signal. The laser frequency is then locked on the frequency corresponding to the maximum of the absorption signal. In this way, the frequency of the laser is *exactly* equal to the frequency of the atomic transition. It is the frequency of the optical clock, whose value will be determined with respect to the primary standard frequency. This will be realized by comparing this optical frequency with the frequency of a cesium primary clock, 40,000 times smaller, using a frequency comb.

The choice of the atomic transition is crucial. In particular, it must allow a narrow absorption line in order to precisely determine the frequency for which absorption is maximal. Consequently, the lifetime of the excited atomic level involved in the clock transition should be long: 1 s corresponds to a natural width of 1 Hz. In the case of the strontium atom, the natural width of the excited level $^3P_0$ is 1 mHz. This implies an additional experimental constraint, because in order to take advantage of this feature we

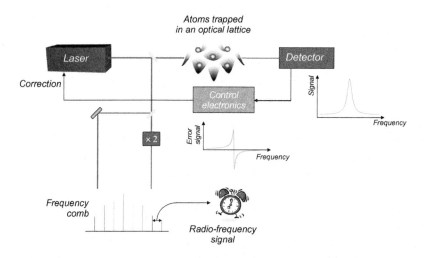

Figure 5.9: Principle of an atomic clock based on atoms trapped in an optical lattice.

should *probe* the atoms for a long time. Typically, atoms in a thermal gas have a mean velocity of about 500 m/s. It is then necessary to slow them, sometimes down to a full stop. Several solutions were proposed to control the motion of atoms and ions — optical traps for example. However, the potential used for trapping induces level shifts and thus inaccuracy of the transition frequency. The Japanese physicist H. Katori proposed an elegant solution for neutral atoms. He showed that using an optical lattice to trap atoms, for given atomic species such as the strontium, there is a magic wavelength which cancels the differential light shift of the clock transition (see the right part of Figure 5.8): the transition frequency is, at first order, exactly the same one as for atoms at rest in the dark (without optical trap). The performance of atomic clocks in the optical domain demonstrated in several laboratories in the world already surpasses that of the cesium clocks in the microwave domain, which leaves no doubt on an upcoming redefinition of the second.

Nowadays, the challenge for physicists in metrology is to build a new international unit system based on a set of fundamental constants. The units will be realized in practice by means of universal standards designed from atomic references and quantum phenomena (for details see C. Bordé, "Base Units of the SI, Fundamental Constants and Modern Quantum Physics", *Phil. Trans. Roy. Soc. A* **363**, 2177 (2005)). The recent advances in physics and the new technologies generated by the laser (laser cooling of neutral atoms, frequency combs, or atom interferometry) will be the key ingredients in this adventure.

5.3.3. *Time transfer with optical fibers*

The impressive progress performed and still under development in the field of time-frequency laser measurements was just presented: laser-cooled atomic clocks from the microwave to the optical spectrum, frequency comparison from radio-frequency until ultraviolet with frequency combs generated by femtosecond lasers. Accuracies of atom or ion frequencies of the order of 10^{-16}. One to two orders of magnitude could be gained during the next decade. Several laboratories develop their own reference system usually not transportable. The key question in metrology is the reliability of the systems and thus the way to compare these different clocks. The GPS system, which is based on conventional cesium clocks, can be used to compare the terrestrial clocks. This has been done but the sensitivity of the comparison is limited by the GPS itself. By averaging the measurements, it takes several days to reach a sensitivity of the comparison of 10^{-15}; the future GALILEO system should not give better results.

An alternative solution has been studied for a few years in France: a 43-km long optical fiber connects the SYRTE (Systèmes de Référence Temps-Espace, Paris Observatory) and the LPL (Laboratoire de Physique des Lasers, Université Paris 13, Villetaneuse) and a reference frequency is sent into this optical fiber. The Paris area is a noisy environment for the optical fiber, and this pollutes this signal. It is thus necessary to correct these perturbations with a feedback-loop. A radio-frequency from 0.1 to 10 GHz (which modulates the laser carrier at 1.55 μm or the laser at 1.55 μm itself) provides the reference frequency. Although this method is entirely satisfactory, it uses a dedicated optical fiber, which is not available between all the laboratories. For that reason, the ultrastable frequency was recently transmitted through the university internet network, coexisting with the common internet traffic. For an optical link of 300 km, the precision of the transmission of the ultrastable frequency is about 10^{-15} after 1 s and 8×10^{-20} after 3 h. This corresponds to a fidelity of the transmission of 0.04 s during the age of the universe, about 13.7 billion years! This is four orders of magnitude better than the GPS and two orders of magnitude better than is required to compare the best distant clocks expected in the next years. Then, it is possible to imagine to build a network of European labs connected by optical fiber. This project is in fact under development with a first objective: the Paris-Braunschweig optical link. To be continued. . .

5.4. Laser Spectroscopy and Tests of Fundamental Physics

5.4.1. *Test of the stability of fundamental constants*

The progress of atomic and molecular clocks, the ability to easily compare very different frequencies and the possibility to transfer ultrastable laser frequencies by optical fiber without degradation allow us to perform experiments unconceivable just a few years ago. This is the case with a test of the time variation of fundamental constants. By definition, a fundamental constant should be constant: for example, the fine structure constant α, the proton-to-electron mass ratio m_p/m_e, etc. This is true in the framework of the standard model of physics. However, this framework is not perfect. For example, General Relativity and Quantum Physics are known to be not fully compatible and several theories have been developed to overcome these difficulties: string theory, supersymmetry, etc. Some of these theories allow the constants to vary over space and time.

Atomic and molecular frequencies depend on a set of fundamental constants. If the values of these constants drift with time, the laser frequency stabilized on one of them should drift as well. In order to observe it, two clocks stabilized on two atomic frequencies which do not imply the same constants must be compared at different moments (usually separated by a few months or years). This has been done between the cesium fountain at SYRTE and a molecular clock involving a vibrational frequency of SF_6, compared thanks to a frequency comb and the optical fiber link between SYRTE and LPL. No variation of the ratio m_p/m_e was detected but the precision of the experiment permitted to claim that such a relative variation is necessarily below 5.6×10^{-14}/year. Future progress in the clock precision should lead to a game-changing situation.

5.4.2. *Test of the isotropy of the speed of light*

The isotropy of the speed of light — the fact that this speed does not depend on the propagation direction — is a consequence of one of the postulates of special relativity. It is therefore another hypothesis that one can consider putting to the test, provided we have a broader theoretical framework where it is not taken for granted.

Let us assume there is a given plane — the horizontal plane in the laboratory in the following — with two preferred directions for which the speed of light does not have its usual value c, but two different values c_1 and c_2. In order to be convincing, demonstrating a violation of the isotropy of the speed of light consists in assigning a nonzero value to $c_1 - c_2$, which means in practice a nonzero value larger than the experimental uncertainty. Many experiments, including one based on GPS propagation delay comparisons, have already been performed, but no one has ever demonstrated any such violation. The physicists simply assigned an upper limit to the violation, corresponding to the smallest value they would have been able to measure: if such a violation exists, they at least demonstrated it is smaller than this value.

Ultrastable lasers allow us to test isotropy in a very simple way, at least at the conceptual level, by simply comparing the resonance frequencies of two linear cavities aligned along the two preferred directions. If we assume that both cavities have exactly the same length L, one will have a free spectral range (frequency interval between two consecutive resonance frequencies) equal to $c_1/2L$, and the other to $c_2/2L$. Measuring the two intervals should yield the value $c_1 - c_2$.

The experiment is actually much harder to implement. The first issue is that physicists have no *a priori* knowledge of the preferred directions — should they exist. The trick is to set both cavities on a rotating table: with any nonzero anisotropy, the frequency difference should then swing back and forth with the same frequency as the rotating motion. But the expected effect is so weak one has to average over a large number of cycles in order to get rid of spurious effects, and then ensure long-term stability of both L_1 and L_2, as one measures $c_1/2L_1$ and c_2/L_2, and certainly not directly c_1 and c_2!

Figure 5.10 presents the principle of such an experiment. A stabilized laser is split into two beams sent into two perpendicular cavities, cut into a single ULE (for *Ultra Low Expansion*) block. Both cavities are then equally sensitive to expansion effects, which are moreover minimized by a temperature feedback of the block, and by its very low expansion coefficient. This allows one to tremendously reduce the fluctuations of the cavity resonance frequencies of thermal origin. These frequencies being *a priori* different, simply tuning the laser frequency is not sufficient to have both cavities simultaneously resonant. One acousto-optic modulator (AOM), which allows to shift the frequency of a laser beam in a controlled manner, is used for each beam. The anisotropy signal is actually searched for into the AOM-driving signals. In a recently performed experiment, the

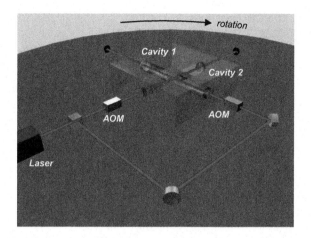

Figure 5.10: Principle of an experimental test of the isotropy of the speed of light. A laser beam is split into two beams sent into two perpendicular cavities. Using the rotation of the experimental apparatus, any anisotropy of c should be seen on the driving signals of the acousto-optic modulators (AOM) which maintain the beams at resonance with both cavities.

rotation period was 90 s, a trade-off between the need to perform as many rotations as possible, and stabilization issues when the table is rotated at high speeds. After one year of data acquisitions (corresponding to 135,000 rotations of the whole experimental apparatus), physicists at Düsseldorf University have not demonstrated any violation, but they have obtained the best upper limit published to this day: $(c_1 - c_2)/2c \leq 10^{-17}$.

5.4.3. Test of parity violation in the spectrum of chiral molecules

A chiral molecule is a molecule which cannot be superimposed to its mirror image. This image is thus another molecule. One of the simplest ones is the CHFClBr molecule, a by-product of methane. These image molecules are called right- and left-handed molecules according to a well-defined nomenclature. Most of the biological molecules are chiral, as amino-acids, sugars, etc. However, with very few exceptions, we only find in nature left amino-acids and right sugars. Why and how has nature made this choice? This is one of the big open scientific questions listed in 2006 in a special issue of *Science* on the occasion of its 125th anniversary.

From the energy viewpoint, image molecules are *a priori* absolutely identical and their spectra should be the same. This is due to the fact that

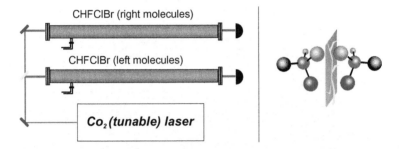

Figure 5.11:   The spectra of two chiral molecules images of each other in a mirror are the same, except if one observes a parity violation effect due to weak interactions. The spectra are recorded simultaneously by using two identical cells. No effect has yet been observed, although a sensitivity of 3×10^{-13} was reached. From C. Daussy *et al.*, *Phys. Rev. Lett.* **83**, 1554 (1999).

the electromagnetic interaction (which is responsible of most of the properties of atoms and molecules) respects the left–right symmetry. Among the four fundamental interactions, only the weak interaction does not, but it has a very short range, of the order of the size of the nuclei, 100,000 smaller than the atoms themselves. Its influence on the molecular spectrum will be extraordinarily weak. However, if there is a deterministic rather than random explanation of this biochirality, there is up to now no other explanation but the very tiny energy difference between right and left molecules.

Because of the weakness of the effect, very few experiments have been performed. One of them is based on very high resolution spectroscopy. The principle consists in recording simultaneously and comparing the spectra of the left and right CHFClBr molecules. By contrast with the usual spectroscopy, the resolution of the experiment is not limited by the linewidth (a few kHz) but by the precision obtained on the line center because the spectra are recorded independently. A resolution of $10\,\text{Hz}$ (3×10^{-13}) was obtained. However, the estimated effect for this molecule is of the order of 10^{-16}! A new project with an expected resolution of 10^{-15} has been designed with new molecules for which the parity violation effect may be of a few 10^{-14}. Laser spectroscopy is pushed to its limits!

5.5.   Distance and Displacement Measurements

5.5.1.   *Telemetry measurements*

As reckless drivers do know, a laser beam can be an efficient tool to measure distances. Binoculars with laser rangefinder indeed use a pulsed laser and a measurement of the roundtrip delay to measure the distance of a car, and its speed by consecutive measurements. Such binoculars mainly use the very low divergence of the beam (of the order of 10^{-3} rad for a 1-mm waist), to accurately target a car tens and even hundreds of meters away. But if such binoculars are rather basic instruments, do you know that more sophisticated ones are routinely used to measure the distance from Earth to the Moon?

One obviously has to adjust the laser. The Moon being about 400,000 km away, the beam divergence has to be further reduced to get a spot of reasonable size on its surface. With a telescope mirror, one gets a waist of 15 cm. After a 400,000-km journey, the beam is now about 1 km in diameter (and even a few km, because of the turbulence it meets in the atmosphere on its way). It is then reflected on retroreflector panels left by Apollo astronauts or Soviet lunar rovers (see Figure 5.12) and is back on track toward Earth. This roundtrip is an energetic nightmare. Over a spot of several square kilometers, only the tiny fraction impinging on the retroreflectors (a few tens of cm wide) is reflected! And again on the returntrip: only photons that finally make it to the telescope mirror are not lost for science! Overall, out of the 10^{19} photons in a laser pulse leaving for the Moon, only 0.1 is detected on average back on Earth! 1 photon every 10 shots! But that photon is quite valuable, since it allows us to measure the Earth–Moon distance with an accuracy of a few millimeters. Astronomers at the Calern site, in the South-East of France (see Figure 5.12) can thus follow its variations, whether they are recurrent (because of the ellipticity

Figure 5.12: Left: Earth–Moon laser station at the Calern site. Right: detail of one of the retroreflectors left on the Moon during one Apollo mission.

of the orbit) or they attest to a drift (typical increase of the order of 3 cm a year, because of tidal effects).

5.5.2. *Interferometric displacement measurements*

This technique however quickly reaches its limits: a 1-mm accuracy requires a timing resolution of a few picoseconds (1 ps $= 10^{-12}$ s). Another technique uses the *phase* of the beam. Figure 5.13 presents the principle of such an experiment: a laser beam is split into two parts by a beamsplitter. The two beams then follow orthogonal paths and experience different phase-shifts, before being recombined on the beamsplitter. The resulting intensity depends on their relative phase: the signal is maximum when both beams are in phase, minimum when they are out of phase, with the laser wavelength λ being the typical length scale. If the length of path 1 is kept constant and if one operates near a working point with a strong signal slope, it is possible to measure variations of the length of path 2 with an accuracy much better than λ.

However, as the beam phase behaves as the second hand of a watch without any minute hand, this method is well suited for length variations (smaller than λ) over time, but certainly not for absolute measurements.

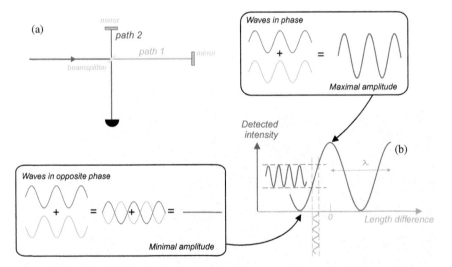

Figure 5.13: Optical interference with a Michelson interferometer. (a) Principle of the interferometer. (b) Detected intensity at the interferometer output with respect to the length difference between the two paths, and application to a displacement measurement. Inserts illustrate the two extreme cases.

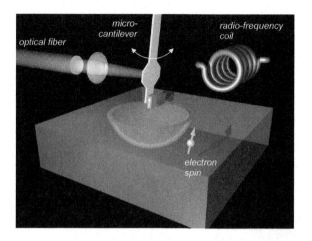

Figure 5.14: Atomic force microscopy setup to mechanically detect the magnetic resonance of a single electron spin, performed at the IBM Research — Almaden laboratory in San Jose, California, in the group of Daniel Rugar. The magnetic resonance is created with a coil (RF coil), which produces a time-varying magnetic field. The cantilever motion is probed by the interference between the beam reflected at the tip of the fiber and the one which propagates to the cantilever.

5.5.3. *How to measure one Ångström*

This technique is so powerful that it allows us to measure displacements smaller than one Ångström (1 Å = 10^{-10} m) with a relatively simple optical setup. Figure 5.14 presents an application of such a sensitive measurement: the measurement of the force exerted over a magnetic sample set at the end of a micro-cantilever (very floppy in order to maximize the induced displacements for a given force). Performed at a temperature of 200 mK, the experiment has allowed to demonstrate a force sensitivity better than one attonewton (1 aN = 10^{-18} N) and to detect the magnetic resonance of a *single electron*. Further progress allows to envision detecting the resonance of a single proton spin (whose magnetic moment is 3 orders of magnitude lower than the electron one), and thereby to visualize the spatial structure of biomolecules.

5.5.4. *How to detect one attometer: the detection of gravitational waves*

If a relatively simple optical setup is good enough to measure displacements at the attometer level, one may wonder if there are more demanding

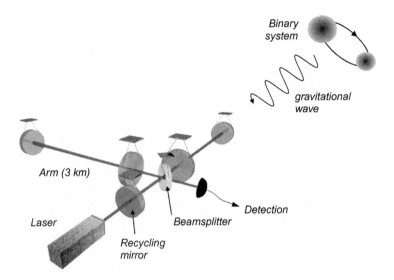

Figure 5.15: The gravitational wave creates an apparent optical length difference between both arms of a km-scale Michelson interferometer. The device sensitivity is increased by the use of Fabry–Perot cavities inside the arms. A recycling mirror sends the reflected light back into the interferometer and allows to increase the available optical power.

experiments in terms of sensitivity and consequently in terms of apparatus sophistication. The answer is positive: the detection of gravitational waves.

These waves are ripples of the curvature of spacetime, predicted by Einstein in 1916, created by huge masses in motion, and that would result in optical length variations. "Would" is actually the right word because no gravitational wave has ever been directly detected. The expected effects are indeed extremely weak: for a device of typical size L, only relative variations $\Delta L/L \simeq 10^{-23}$ are expected on Earth, even for astrophysical events as cataclysmic as the merger of two black holes.

Some projects are currently trying to detect such events, for example near Pisa for the French-Italian cooperation Virgo or in the US for Ligo. These are gigantic instruments: the Michelson interferometer has km-long arms, with optical cavities embedded in which light makes several roundtrips to increase their effective lengths. To minimize parasitic fluctuations, mirrors are suspended in vacuum by a complex insulation system. The ultrastable laser source then allows to detect variations ΔL of the order of 10^{-20} m, at the limit where events are likely to happen.

Chapter 6

Photons and Atoms

Michèle Leduc

CNRS Senior Researcher,
Laboratoire Kastler Brossel, Paris, France

Nicolas Treps

Professor, Université Pierre et Marie Curie,
Laboratoire Kastler Brossel, Paris, France

The first chapter of this book showed that laser light is coherent light concentrated in a given mode of radiation resonant with the optical cavity. This property makes laser light the "cleanest" light that physicists are able to produce, and it is thus quite naturally that the laser, an outcome of fundamental research with multiple applications, made its comeback into laboratories as being itself an object of research. We shall not review here all the advances in fundamental physics resulting from the use of laser light (the interested reader may consult the book by Michel Le Bellac in the same series), but we wish to explain through examples why the approach based on wave-particle duality is particularly fruitful.

This duality influences not only intrinsic properties of light, such as they may be measured in laboratories, but also applications where light is used as a measurement tool or for communications. Laser light is composed of photons, whose spatial and temporal distributions induce unavoidable fluctuations in intensity and direction. These are the properties which we are going to study, while showing how it is possible to make use of the particle character of light in order to improve high sensitivity measurements.

On the other hand, this duality allows us to revisit atom–light interaction. It allows us to understand atom cooling at temperatures so low that a new state of matter could be discovered, namely Bose–Einstein condensates.

In this latter case, it is wave-particle duality of matter that is at work! Today, these properties find applications in metrology, in particular, in the design of clocks of unprecedented accuracy.

6.1. Laser Light, a Well-Ordered Light?

6.1.1. *Lasers and photons*

The first chapter of this book invoked both aspects of light in order to explain the operation of the laser. First of all, light is a wave, which allows us to understand the resonances of the optical cavity and the selection of the mode of operation. On the other hand, light is composed of particles, which allows us to explain its coherent amplification by atoms. However, this latter feature seems to be a rather *ad hoc* description of matter–light interaction: does the photon have an intrinsic existence?

A first answer was already given in this book, illustrated in Figure 5.12, namely the measurement of the Earth–Moon distance. One explains there that the energy of the light pulse which comes back from the Moon and is incident on the detector is less than one-tenth of the energy of a single photon. Now, it is not possible to split a photon. What kind of object is then detected? The detector registers on average one photon every 10 shots, which is consistent with both the average power predicted theoretically and the indivisible character of the photon: quantum physics is a probabilistic theory, where the average power is replaced by the probability to measure a photon. This is what is experimentally observed! The concept of a photon has been around for some time now, as its theoretical existence was introduced by Einstein in 1905, and it is an indivisible quantum of energy whose value E_γ is $E_\gamma = h\nu = \hbar\omega$ with $\hbar = h/2\pi \simeq 10^{-34}$ J.s where $\omega = 2\pi\nu$ is the angular frequency of the light wave.

Very famous experiments allowed physicists to directly highlight both the wave-particle duality and the probabilistic character of quantum theory. The reader is referred to specialized texts to learn more on the subject. The laser allowed us to directly perform some of these experiments. Let us quote here the generation of single photons. Actually, it is possible to generate one photon, and only one, thanks to the remarkable properties of the interaction between a laser and a nonlinear medium. Nonlinear effects were already addressed in Chapters 4 and 5, and it was shown in particular that they lead to the mixing of different frequencies which results, for example, in the creation of new ones. In fact, nonlinear effects induce interactions between several waves of different frequencies in such a way that, due to energy conservation, the sum of the frequencies of the primary beams is equal to the sum of the frequencies of the generated beams, where the number of beams which are involved depends on the kind of nonlinearity.

Let us now consider the second-order nonlinearity of order two, where a beam called the pump beam (p) generates in a crystal two beams called *signal* (s) and *idler* (i), such that $\omega_p = \omega_s + \omega_i$. Moreover, to ensure the phases of the different beams remain coherent along the propagation direction in the crystal, a relation termed phase matching must hold, in such a way that $\vec{k}_p = \vec{k}_s + \vec{k}_i$, where $\vec{k} = (n\omega/c)\vec{u}$ is the light wave vector, whose magnitude depends on the angular frequency ω and on the optical index n of the medium, while $\vec{u}$ is a unit vector oriented along the propagation direction. All these constraints taken together imply that for a given pump beam, many pairs of beams with different signal and idler frequencies may be emitted, but the colors effectively emitted are direction dependent and thus form cones, as can be seen in Figure 6.1.

Let us return to our photons. It is quite remarkable that the relation between light frequencies is translated into a relation between photon energies, since it is equivalent to $\hbar\omega_p = \hbar\omega_s + \hbar\omega_i$. It thus amounts to splitting a pump photon, which gives birth to a signal photon and an idler photon, as illustrated in Figure 6.1. Measurement of the signal photon allows us to check the presence of an idler photon, and it is precisely this configuration which allowed physicists to perform a number of experiments hinging

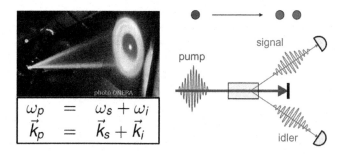

Figure 6.1: Generation of heralded single photons: in the upper graph, a pulsed laser beam is incident on a nonlinear crystal and generates several *signal* and *idler* pairs according to the relation written below the picture. The emitted colors depend on the propagation direction, and one observes light cones. In the right-hand graph, the pump pulse has a low power, so that it only emits one pair of photons. The detection of one photon in the signal channel ensures that one photon, and only one, is present in the idler channel.

on single photons, and in particular experiments for one- and two-photons interferences. It is also at the origin of a new field of research: quantum information, since in particular these sources allowed the first demonstrations of quantum cryptography.

6.1.2. Light noise

The laser has been at the basis of many advances in physics, and particularly in metrology, as is explained in Chapter 5. The accuracies which are reached are remarkable, but how far can we go? The ultimate accuracy of measurements performed with a laser is governed by the quantum nature of light, as in the case of the measurement of the Earth–Moon distance. Let us, for example, analyze a simple measurement of laser intensity with a photodiode. If the laser could be perfectly stabilized, the intensity which is delivered would be constant. However, a measurement performed with a very accurate photodiode still displays fluctuations of this intensity: it is the random arrival times of the photons which generate these tiny fluctuations, as can be seen in the upper part of Figure 6.2.

How do these fluctuations influence the accuracy of optical measurements? In practice, with a perfectly stabilized laser, while the mean value of the intensity is well-defined, photons are still randomly distributed in time: they follow a statistical law called the Poisson law. This law states that, if in each measurement we know that the average number of photons

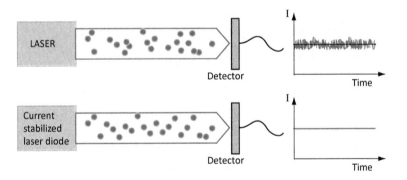

Figure 6.2: Photon distribution in a light beam. In the upper graph, for a standard laser, photons are randomly distributed and induce fluctuations when light intensity is measured. In the lower graph, the instants of emission of photons by a laser diode follow the statistics of the power supply, and fluctuations vanish during measurement.

is N, then the number of photons in the measurement will lie between $N - 2\sqrt{N}$ and $N + 2\sqrt{N}$ with 95% probability. Thus, the larger the average number of photons, the weaker the relative fluctuations, and therefore quantum fluctuations will influence the quality of the measurement less.

Let us give some orders of magnitude. Consider a laser pointer with a power on the order of 1 milliwatt. If this pointer emits green light with a 532 nm wavelength λ, then $\omega = 2\pi c/\lambda \simeq 3.5 \times 10^{15}$ rad/s. The corresponding photon energy is $E_\gamma = \hbar\omega \simeq 3.5 \times 10^{-19}$ J. Since $1\,\text{mW}=10^{-3}$ J/s, a 1 mW laser diode corresponds to a photon flux of about 10^{15} photons per second. If one measures this beam for 1 s, the relative fluctuations will be on the order of 10^{-8} and seem to be negligibly small, except for the high sensitivity experiments described in Chapter 5. Moreover, one clearly sees in Figure 6.3 that, as soon as the number of photons goes down to about a few thousands, relative fluctuations are large and perturb the measurement sensitivity.

Is this photon noise unassailable? The Poissonian noise in standard lasers is due to the randomness of emission times in the amplifying medium. Were it possible to control this noise, then it could be reduced. Now, in the case of the laser diodes described in Section 2.2.3, we explained that the electrical current supplied to the semiconductor medium implies photon emission. Some media have an efficiency such that, in practice, each electron of the current will give rise to the emission of one photon. Now, it is quite possible to control the statistics of the electrons in the current (in practice, it is enough to cool the power supply down, as fluctuations have essentially a thermal origin), and thus to directly control the statistics of the emitted photons. This is called the principle of the *quiet pumping*, which allows the laser diode to emit *sub-poissonian* light, and thus to improve the signal-to-noise ratio of measurements, as illustrated in the lower graph of Figure 6.2.

There exist in fact many techniques allowing to control the statistics of fluctuations of quantum origin present in the light emitted by a laser, and this control is the subject of numerous research projects. Processes based on the *quiet pumping* principle are not the most efficient ones, and researchers preferentially use nonlinear effects (such as those illustrated in Figure 6.1) in order to manipulate photon statistics. It has recently been possible to obtain beams whose quantum fluctuations are smaller than those of a standard laser, and this kind of beam has recently been used in gravitational waves detectors, in order to improve their sensitivity (see Section 5.5.4).

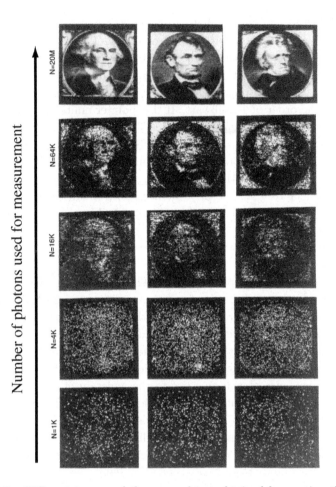

Figure 6.3: Different images of the same object obtained by varying the total number of photons in the experiment. One observes that, the smaller the number of photons, the more important the relative noise, and the worse the image definition (After Morris in *Optical Processes and Computing*, H. H. Arsenault, T. Szoplik and B. Macukow editors, Academic New York, p. 343).

6.1.3. *Straight line propagation of light?*

Another fundamental property of light may be revisited from the perspective of its particle nature: its propagation direction. Indeed, in classical physics, light propagates in vacuum following a straight line, by definition. This property continues to hold true in special relativity, but the situation becomes more complicated in general relativity, where space-time is curved

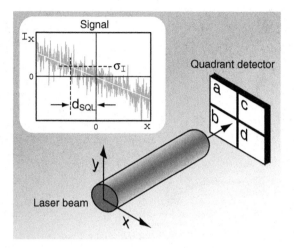

Figure 6.4: Measurement with great accuracy of the position of a laser beam performed by comparing the incident powers on the various detectors. Inset: by computing $(a + b) - (c + d)$, one obtains a signal proportional to the horizontal position, but the smallest measurable shift d_{SQL} is limited by fluctuations of quantum origin.

by gravity and light follows curved trajectories; however, these are precisely the null geodesics, the equivalent of the shortest connection between two locations.

Is it possible to accurately measure the propagation direction of light, its pointing direction? This is proposed in Figure 6.4, which illustrates a very simple technique used in many measurement apparatuses. If the laser beam is incident on a quadrant detector, the comparison between incident powers on the different pixels allows us to precisely know the beam position with respect to the detector.

For example, if we wish to know the horizontal position of the beam, we may compute the difference between the power incident on the left hand part of the detector, $(a + b)$, and that incident on the right hand part, $(c + d)$. This difference vanishes if the beam is perfectly centered. Otherwise, it is proportional to the horizontal shift. Now, the beam is composed of photons, which are randomly distributed not only in time, but also in space (as in Figure 6.2). This implies that, even if the beam is perfectly centered, one does not exactly find the same number of photons on the two halves of the detector and, once more, the value of the difference fluctuates. As is seen in the inset of Figure 6.4, the signal associated with the difference is no longer a straight line, but it is subject to fluctuations

Figure 6.5: Photograph of an optical cavity which allows one to modify quantum fluctuations of light. The cavity is made of four mirrors and the crystal is located in a copper oven in order to control its temperature (Australian Center for Quantum-Atom Optics).

which limit the measurement accuracy; this noise is termed the quantum noise limit, and is proportional to the square root of the number of photons. Because of quantum physics, the pointing direction of light fluctuates! For example, in the case of a few milliwatts laser beam with a diameter of a few hundred micrometers, it fluctuates by a few Ångströms every microsecond.

By using experimental techniques illustrated in Figure 6.5, it is in fact possible to order photons in time and space, and to improve, in principle, the pointing noise of a laser beam. This approach can be generalized to any measurement of great accuracy which is limited by quantum fluctuations of light and, even if it is at present confined within research laboratories because of the difficulties in controlling photons, the possible applications to metrology and to fundamental physics make this field of research a very active one.

6.2.   Using Lasers for Cold Atom Physics

6.2.1.   *Photons slow atoms down*

We saw in Chapter 1 that atoms have discrete energy levels and can absorb photons carried by a light beam, provided that the energy $h\nu$ of the photons is just equal to the distance between levels E_1 and E_2 ($h\nu = E_2 - E_1$). But photons carry not only energy, they also carry momentum $p = h\nu/c = \hbar k$, where k is the modulus of the light wave vector. The photon flux of the light

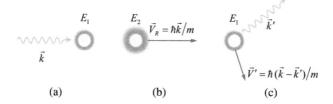

(a) (b) (c)

Figure 6.6: Absorption/emission cycle of a photon by an atom. In (a) the atom is at rest in its ground state of energy E_1. It catches a photon coming from a given direction. In (b) it is excited to the E_2 state with a velocity $\vec{V}_R$ in the direction of the incident beam. In (c) it falls back in the E_1 ground state and emits a photon in a random direction.

beam is thus able to transfer this momentum to matter. The momentum transfer per time unit generates a force. Such a force per surface unit results in the so-called radiation pressure. Initially at rest, the atom absorbs a photon as shown in Figure 6.6(a). It gets a momentum $\hbar\vec{k}$ and takes a velocity $\vec{V}_R = \hbar\vec{k}/m$, where m is the atom mass. Such a velocity, called recoil velocity, is directed along the beam, as shown in Figure 6.6(b). This process can be figured out by thinking of a goalkeeper's recoil when he receives the momentum carried by the ball he catches. The wavelength of the light bringing the atom from the ground state to the first excited state is $\lambda = 589\,\text{nm}$ if one deals with sodium. The recoil velocity of the sodium atom after absorption of the photon is about $3\,\text{cm/s}$.

It was shown in Chapter 1 that the atom, once brought up to the E_2 excited state, quickly falls back to its ground state through spontaneous emission of a new photon after a very short time, typically $3 \times 10^{-8}\,\text{s}$ for the sodium atom. It simultaneously loses the momentum transmitted by the incident photon and carried away by the re-emitted photon. But if the absorbed photons always carry a momentum in a direction fixed by the incident laser, the photons resulting from the spontaneous emission are emitted in a random direction, as shown in Figure 6.6(c). Let us assume that a beam of atoms propagating in a given direction meets a counter propagating laser beam. The atoms undergo absorption/emission cycles many times per second, so that the total momentum carried away by the re-emitted photons vanishes on average. The net result is that the atoms catch momentum always in the same direction and after a large number of absorption/emission cycles, they end up being strongly slowed down. For a sodium atom the resulting deceleration is of order of $10^6\,\text{m/s}^2$, namely a hundred thousand times larger than the gravity acceleration.

It is not a surprise that such an extremely large deceleration by light allows
to stop an atomic beam over a short distance, usually shorter than 1 meter.
The atomic velocity changes from a few hundred m/s at room temperature
down to a few cm/s. It is expected that the lowest velocity one can reach
is the recoil velocity V_R. However, using the refined properties of quantum mechanics, physicists were able to go beyond such recoil barrier and
to lower the temperature even further down. Claude Cohen-Tannoudji at
Ecole Normale Supérieure in Paris played a major role in the understanding
of such processes in the 80's.

One must add a precision to the previous explanation: during the slowing process, the absorption frequency of the laser by the atoms changes
due to Doppler effect. The laser frequency being fixed, in order to maintain the atoms in resonance with the laser so that they keep absorbing
the counter propagating photons, the most common method is the *Zeeman slower*, invented by William Phillips: the atomic beam travels along
a magnet delivering a magnetic field spatially variable which shifts the
atomic energy levels depending on the field. The $E_2 - E_1$ atomic splitting
constantly keeps in resonance with the laser frequency as the Zeeman effect
compensates the Doppler effect.

It has just been shown that one can stop an atomic beam nearly completely with a counter propagating light beam. It remains to explain how
one can simultaneously decrease its temperature. Let us recall that the
concept of temperature is related to the spread of the particle velocity.
The cooling principle is based on the Doppler effect. Atoms whose resonance frequency is ν, with $h\nu = E_2 - E_1$, are shown in Figure 6.7. They are
located between two laser beams propagating in opposite directions. The
laser frequency is chosen slightly below ν. Thanks to the Doppler effect,

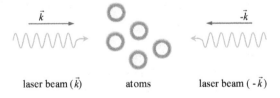

laser beam ($\vec{k}$)   atoms   laser beam (-$\vec{k}$)

Figure 6.7: Principle of laser cooling of a gas by Doppler effect in one dimension. Atoms are located between two laser beams, frequency detuned from the
resonance. Because of the Doppler effect, if an atom moves to the right it absorbs
the beam coming from the right more than the one coming from the left. The
resulting friction force slows the atoms down and confines them at the center of
the figure.

left moving atoms get closer to resonance with the laser beam coming from the left. On the other hand, they run even further from resonance with the beam coming from the right. Consequently, they prefer absorbing photons coming from the left than from the right and thus they slow down. For right moving atoms the role of the two light beams is reversed and the atoms are equally slowed down. In first approximation they are submitted to a force proportional to their velocity, analogous to a friction force. If one displays a pair of counter propagating beams in the three directions in space, one can decrease the thermal motion and reach temperatures of the order of 100 μK. Actually, experiments showed that temperatures even lower than the theoretical limit of Doppler cooling could be reached. When trying to solve this intriguing phenomenon physicists discovered other cooling mechanisms.

6.2.2. *Trapping atoms with laser beams*

Even if laser light allows slowing and cooling of atoms, one actually needs to keep them long enough at the same place to be able to study them. One can first think of using the above described friction force of the laser beams on the atoms. With three pairs of red detuned counter-propagating light beams, atoms are submitted to a friction force as soon as them move; they are pushed by Doppler effect to the focusing point of the beams and trapped there with very slow velocity. They seem to be glued in the beam lattice as in a honey pot: this is called an *optical molasse*. The first optical molasses were demonstrated by Steven Chu in the late 70's. They kept a cloud of cold atoms levitating in vacuum, preventing them from hitting the cell walls for a few seconds. The three physicists Claude Cohen-Tannoudji, William Philips, and Steven Chu, shown in Figure 6.8, were awarded the Nobel Prize in 1997 for the laser cooling and trapping of atoms.

Yet trapping atoms in optical molasses is not enough for experiments, as the friction force keeping the atoms up is just an average. Each atom has a randomly fluctuating trajectory due to successive absorption and emission of photons; it ends up escaping from the optical molasse after a few seconds. In order to increase the confinement time of the atoms, it was requested to invent other trapping methods taking advantage of a restoring force.

Various types of traps have been implemented. The oldest and most commonly used one is the magneto-optical trap, whose principle was formulated by Jean Dalibard in 1988. It is based on optical pumping methods in use for decades in the laboratory founded by Alfred Kastler and Jean Brossel. The idea is to add an inhomogeneous magnetic field to the optical

Claude   Steven   Williams
Cohen-Tannoudji   Chu   Phillips

Figure 6.8:   The three laureates who were awarded the 1997 physics Nobel Prize
for the discovery of methods to cool and trap atoms with laser light: Claude
Cohen-Tannoudji at Ecole Normale Supérieure in Paris, Steven Chu at Stanford
University and William Phillips at NIST in the United States.

molasse and to make use of polarized light. As a result, a restoring force
pushes the atoms towards the center of the molasse. Such magneto-optical
traps are able to confine billions of atoms for several minutes. Figure 6.9
shows the fluorescence of a strontium atomic gas levitating in a magneto-
optical trap imaged through the windows of the container keeping ultra
high vacuum. The cloud size is of millimetric order. Another trapping
method is based on the changes of the atomic energy levels induced by
optical fields, also called *light shifts*. A rather intense laser beam is focused
at the center of the vacuum cell; its frequency is significantly lower than
the atomic resonance frequency. The light shifts induced by the laser create a potential well for the cold atoms which accumulate close the beam
focusing point. Such purely optical traps are more and more in use. They
offer several advantages if compared to magneto-optical traps, namely they
require no magnetic field and make use of commercially available lasers
whose frequency can be strongly detuned from the atomic resonance.

Combining two interfering laser beams, one can obtain a light field periodically oscillating in space. A remarkable result is that the atoms can be
trapped in such a regular lattice of potential wells. With three pairs of
counter-propagating beams, one creates a so-called 3D optical lattice in
which the atoms find themselves trapped in adjacent sites separated by a
nanometric distance, as if stored inside an egg box (see an artistic view in
Figure 6.10). Cold atoms regularly displayed in optical lattices are quite
analogous to electrons in a crystal where the periodical potential is created

Figure 6.9: A magneto-optical trap of cold strontium atoms at the center a vacuum chamber. The atomic cloud is visualized through fluorescence (from Pierre Lemonde, SYRTE laboratory at Paris Observatory).

by the ions. They are now used as model systems for condensed matter physics, with the advantage that their significant parameters are adjustable at will. They allow studying very complex phenomena such as superconductivity, this amazing property shown by some materials which can transport electrical current without losses. With another geometry of the laser beams creating the optical lattice, one can also order the atoms in a different geometry, in analogy with matter in dimension one or two. Figure 6.10 shows two pairs of counter-propagating laser beams creating *tubes* of cold atoms.

6.2.3. *The Bose–Einstein condensation and the atom lasers*

The spectacular methods of laser cooling of atoms promptly triggered even more astonishing discoveries, such as the possibility to bring a dilute gas down to temperatures extremely low, close to the absolute zero, while keeping the sample in a gaseous state. This can be viewed as a true paradox, as in general all gases turn into liquids below a given temperature, for example 77 K for nitrogen or 4 K for helium. Yet a very intriguing phenomenon called Bose–Einstein condensation was predicted in 1925 by Albert Einstein who developed an idea of the Indian physicist Satyendra Nath Bose. Note

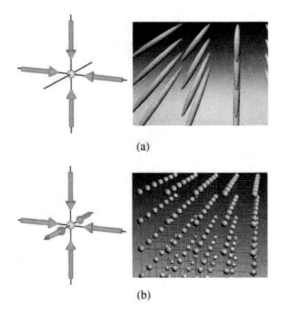

(a)

(b)

Figure 6.10: Trapping cold atoms in optical lattices. Pairs of counter-propagating laser beams generate standing waves resulting in periodical potentials in which atoms can be trapped. (a) 2D lattice; (b) 3D lattice.

that one does not deal here with a gas–liquid phase transition but with atom accumulation in the ground state of a trap. The two physicists predicted that in a gas of identical noninteracting atoms, new effects could occur at low temperature, provided the density is high enough: the ensemble of atoms contained in the trap could collectively behave as if they were a single atom. To understand that, one needs to refer to a basic notion of quantum mechanics: any particle can be described by a wave, whose spatial spread is characterized by a wavelength λ_{dB}, called the de Broglie wavelength after the name of the French physicist who first made this fundamental quantum prediction. λ_{dB} is exceedingly small at room temperature, but it increases when the gas cools down, as it is proportional to the inverse of the square root of temperature.

The de Broglie wavelength, λ_{dB}, can be compared to the mean distance, d, between the gas particles in a cell (see Figure 6.11). At room temperature, λ_{dB} is much smaller than the distance d between the atoms, which collide into each other as billiard balls under the influence of thermal agitation. But if the temperature is sufficiently lowered, λ_{dB} may turn out

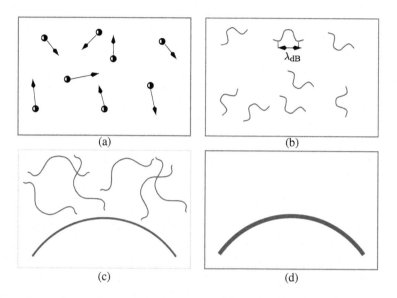

Figure 6.11:   Principle of the Bose–Einstein condensation. The de Broglie wavelength λ_{dB} associated with each particle increases when the temperature is lowered from (a) to (b). In (a) at room temperature the particles behave like billiard balls. In (b) λ_{dB} is of the order of d, the mean distance between particles. In (d) close to absolute zero only a unique wave function remains. The Bose–Einstein condensation appears in (c) and is complete in (d).

to be of the same order as d and the de Broglie waves of the particles overlap. At a given temperature T_C depending on the gas density, a fraction of the atoms can be collectively described by a unique wave; they accumulate in the ground state of the trap, being in the same quantum state of minimum energy. This phenomenon is called condensation, even though the system goes on being a very dilute gas. The lower the temperature goes below T_C, the larger the condensed fraction of the gas. Such phase transition is of purely quantum origin. The idea of the Bose–Einstein condensation of gases remained for long unexploited as it requires extremely low temperatures to show up. For instance, in a cell filled with rubidium gas at a few millibars, the distance d is of order a few μm; λ_{dB} only turns to the same order of magnitude as d at temperature below the μK range, meaning a millionth of a degree above absolute zero.

The field became increasingly topical when one started to know how to cool and trap atoms with lasers. The first experimental evidence for the Bose–Einstein condensation was achieved in 1995 with rubidium atoms by Eric Cornell and Carl Wieman in Boulder, Colorado. They were soon followed by Wolgang Ketterle with sodium atoms at MIT in Cambridge, Massachusetts. The three physicists were awarded the Nobel prize in 2002 for this major discovery. To reach this goal, they had to invent an additional cooling method in order to lower the temperature very much below that provided by the above described magneto-optical traps. This method is called *evaporative cooling*, most currently operated in a purely magnetic trap. It consists in progressively getting rid of the hottest atoms, in a way looking like cooling a hot liquid by blowing on it. The particles carrying the largest energy tend to escape from the trap. The trap depth is progressively decreased while the thermal equilibrium keeps established at each step. In this way, the temperature is pulled down to the critical temperature of the Bose–Einstein condensation. One can produce macroscopic samples of gaseous condensates containing a few million atoms.

Figure 6.12 shows the image of a sodium condensate obtained at MIT. The observation is carried out with optical methods by recording the absorption of a probe laser beam which crosses the atomic cloud (see for instance the three black and white pictures at the top of Figure 6.12). The bottom part of the figure displays the reconstructed velocity distribution

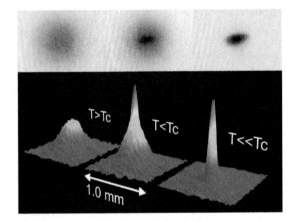

Figure 6.12: Bose–Einstein condensation of sodium. The image is a 2D reconstruction of the atomic velocity spread when temperature goes down. On the left side, the temperature is above condensation; the velocity distribution is that of a normal gas. In the center, the temperature is just slightly below the critical temperature for condensation. On the right side, nearly all the gas has undergone the Bose–Einstein condensation (photo Wolfgang Ketterle, MIT-USA).

in two dimensions. Above the critical temperature T_C, the velocity distribution is that of a gas in thermal equilibrium. As soon as the temperature gets close to T_C, a narrower peak shows up at the center of the distribution, related to the fraction of atoms which have condensed in the ground state of the trap. Much below T_C, nearly all the atoms have condensed. One can think of extracting them from the trap where they are confined. This can be obtained by creating a *leak* in the trap: atoms fall off as a beam under gravity and keep all the properties they had in the condensate over a certain distance. They all travel in the same direction, with the same energy and the same velocity. Such atomic beams can be described as coherent matter wave packets propagating in space. They show many similarities with the optical lasers extensively discussed in this book. This is why they are called *atom lasers*. An atom laser is shown in Figure 6.13, here optically guided in order to force a horizontal trajectory. Atom lasers can be manipulated like usual lasers, showing properties similar to the optical ones such as reflection from a surface, deflection, splitting in two and interference. If one remembers how much time was needed for the laser to find its applications after its discovery, one takes no risk at predicting a brilliant future for the atom laser...

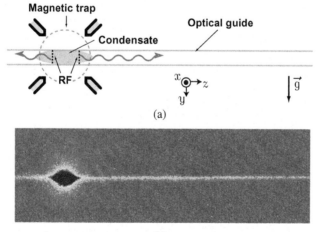

(b)

Figure 6.13: An atom laser is extracted from a Bose–Einstein condensate kept in a *leaking* magnetic trap. An optical guide prevents it from falling under gravity. The so-called RF knife is used to decouple some atoms from the trap (photo Vincent Josse, Laboratoire Charles Fabry, Palaiseau, France).

Today, Bose–Einstein condensates can be produced with a collection of diverse atoms: sodium, rubidium, potassium, cesium, strontium, calcium, the helium atom in a metastable state, hydrogen, some rare earth atoms such as ytterbium, some metals such as chromium. Furthermore, one can condensate molecules of alkali dimers by controlling at will the interaction forces between ultracold atoms with magnetic fields. The condensate gallery increases every year. The research domain that they opened up is now exploding all over the world with experiments and theory, which unexpectedly bring closer atomic and condensed matter physics.

6.2.4.   *Clocks of amazing precision...*

One could think that gases cooled to so such extremely low temperature will have only a curiosity value. Actually, they have already allowed spectacular breakthroughs in fundamental physics. For instance, the domain of atomic spectroscopy has been renewed by the tight control of the atom velocity. The subsequently improved determination of the energy levels provides relevant comparisons with the most elaborate theoretical predictions (see Section 6.5). Yet this is not the only interest of cold atoms. In fact, they have already found some practical applications which will be more and more exploited in industry.

The most important one deals with atomic clocks whose principle is described in Section 5.3.2. One knows that the most precise method for measuring time is to use the frequency of a transition between two atomic levels and to compare it to the frequency of a quartz oscillator. The time standard is based on the cesium atom for which the relevant transition is in the microwave domain. The precision of such a measurement depends on its duration. In a usual clock operated at room temperature, atoms travel at a velocity of a few hundred meters per second. Between the interrogation zones, the duration of the measurement is in the millisecond range, as it is limited by the finite size of the system. But if one turns to cold atoms traveling at velocities of the order of $1\,\text{m/s}$, for instance extracted from a magneto-optical trap, the measurement can be operated for a much longer time. One can thus obtain much narrower lines and gain on the precision of their positioning.

Figure 6.14 shows a cold atom fountain clock. A cloud of sodium atoms is kept levitating in a vacuum at the center of a magneto-optical trap whose six laser beams are represented. The atoms are kicked up by a laser pulse and then fall back down under gravity acceleration. The optical detection

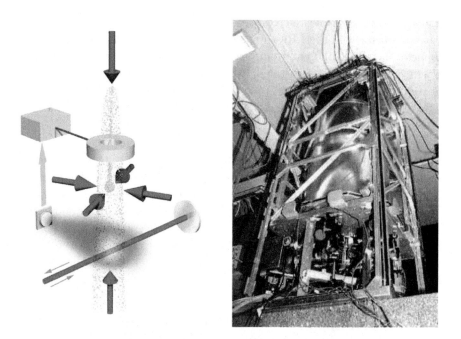

Figure 6.14: The cold atom fountain clock. Atoms levitating at the center of a magneto-optical trap are pushed upwards by a laser pulse, then they fall back under gravity. They cross twice the measurement radiofrequency cavity represented by a green ring. The optical detection operates through the absorption of a laser probe beam (Christophe Salomon's sketch on the left). On the right, the cesium fountain clock at Observatoire de Paris (picture by André Clairon).

is operated through the absorption of a laser beam probing the atoms after their travel up and down. This arrangement shows similarities with a water beam in a fountain. The atomic beam crosses twice, first going up, second going down, the radiofrequency interrogation zone represented by a ring in Figure 6.14. The duration of the measurement is the time elapsed between the travels up and down of the atomic beam, typically of the order of one second for atoms extracted from a trap at $4\,\mu$K. The gain in precision is about 100 over conventional clocks at room temperature. One reaches a stability of the order of 10^{-14} in 1 s and even better for longer times. The relative accuracy of fountain clocks now reaches a few 10^{-16}, meaning approximately 1 s over 100 million years. Figure 6.14 shows the sodium fountain clock of the SYRTE laboratory at Paris Observatory. It is several meters high and has been for years the most precise clock in the world. Nowadays, over 30 such clocks have been built or are under construction.

They provide the time reference in their geographic zone and communicate between each other. Research goes on and new clocks are developing. Some of them use different atoms such as strontium, ytterbium or mercury, operating on transitions in the optical rather than microwave domain (see Section 5.3.2). It is expected that they will provide an even better precision. The definition of the second might very well change in the future with the replacement of cesium by another atom.

Is it likely that the technology used for time measurement has nearly reached its limits? Not yet. There remains another idea to exploit: launching the clock in space. The fountain concept can be transposed for a microgravity environment, leading to a clock where the measurement duration will be even further increased. Such a space clock is under development with the PHARAO program of CNES (National Center for Space Studies) and should be launched to the international space platform in 2015, as shown in Figure 6.15. It will be compared to other types of highly stable clocks such as a hydrogen maser, also attached to the space platform.

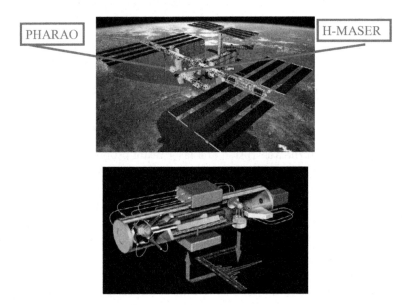

Figure 6.15: The PHARAO program for a clock in space, showing its positioning on the international space platform. The sketch of the PHARAO cavity shows atoms confined in a magneto-optical trap on the left, traveling in straight line to the right, interrogated through two distinct zones and ultimately optically detected on the right. In red the interference signal which is expected.

It will provide a unique reference of time to all the clocks on earth. Very fundamental physics measurements are also planned with the cold atom space clock, such as tests of Einstein's general relativity.

Can one expect less sophisticated applications of cold atoms? A large number of groups are trying. One way is to miniaturize the devices by inserting them on the so-called atom-chips of micrometer dimensions, where electrical currents running through wires produce the necessary trapping magnetic fields. Chip-clocks are on the way, integrating both the atom trap and the lasers on the same chip. Cold atom clocks might one day fit out satellites for more precise time reference and positioning in the GPS system. And when shall we wear cold atom watches?

Other cold atom based instruments such as gyroscopes are currently under study. Their principle is introduced in Section 6.3. They are on use for the positioning of planes and ships. When matter waves replace optical waves in such instruments, one expects a spectacular gain in precision. Technological challenges are high, research intensifies, atoms lasers and optical lasers are neck to neck. The adventure of cold atoms is just starting.

Chapter 7

Medical Applications

A. Claude Boccara

Professor, ESPCI-Paris Tech,
Institut Langevin, Laboratoire d'Optique,
Paris, France

Serge Mordon

Research Director — Professor INSERM
Lille University Hospital
Lille, France

In re-listening to the lectures of Charles Townes shortly after the invention of the laser (e.g., in the Boston Science Museum), one can already have a realistic vision of the potentialities of this new tool in the field of medical therapy, as evidenced by the use of the laser in ophthalmology to cure retinal detachment in the 1960's.

Since then, applications have flourished in the domain of therapy. We will thus illustrate here only some of the main fields of application of medical lasers.

On the opposite, the use of lasers in medical imaging is, with one exception in ophthalmology, still at the development level. It is becoming a diagnostic tool in addition to high performance imaging facilities that are often very expensive (such as CT scan, Magnetic Resonance Imaging (MRI) and nuclear imaging). Even if progress is sometimes slow, one can now image with light inside the human body, in spite of the strong scattering of light by tissues, in the same way as a pathologist sees surgical specimens.

7.1. Laser and Therapy

7.1.1. *Introduction*

7.1.1.1. *History*

Since their invention in 1960, lasers have emerged as potentially interesting light sources for medicine because they possessed three characteristics that set them apart from conventional sources: directivity, the ability to operate in pulsed mode with very short pulses and monochromaticity. This latter property is without doubt the least useful in medicine because biological molecules have an extended absorption spectrum and their activation does not require a source which is spectrally very narrow.

Medical applications are going to be found very quickly with this new instrument. The ruby laser had been used since 1961 by Campbell in ophthalmology and by Goldman in dermatology in 1963. Then, the argon ion laser (488–514 nm) quickly became the laser of choice for the treatment of retinal detachment. The carbon dioxide laser (CO_2), introduced by Polanyi in 1965 and Kaplan in 1967, had been first of all proposed to surgeons with the concept of an "optical" scalpel. It has since been implemented in very numerous applications, most especially dermatology. The use of optical fibers in the course of the 1970s opened the field of endocavitary laser applications thanks to the possibility of introducing the fiber into the working channel of an endoscope. Still here, the argon laser (Dwyer in 1975), but especially the neodymium YAG laser (Kiefhaber in 1975), have been used in gastroenterology, in pulmonology. In 1976, Hofstetter employed the laser for the first time in urology. Thanks to the dye laser, the end of the 1970's saw the rapid expansion of photodynamic therapy (Dougherty, 1976).

Since the beginning of 1980's, laser applications have been particularly developed. Having become an essential tool in ophthalmology, the laser conquered other disciplines and the field never ceases to evolve. Certain indications disappear in favor of other techniques whilst new applications regularly emerge.

In 2010, the ASLMS (American Society for Laser in Medicine and Surgery) and SFLM (Société Francophone des Lasers Médicaux), the French Society for Medical Lasers, celebrated their 30 years of existence, witnessing the vitality of a discipline with continuous growth, as much in terms of the diversification of applications as in the number of patients treated.

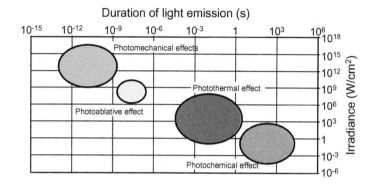

Figure 7.1: The different effects induced by lasers depending on the duration of laser emission and the irradiance (S. Mordon).

7.1.1.2. *Principle*

Therapeutic applications of lasers exploit a certain number of effects that can be produced by the action of a light beam on a biological tissue. Whatever the effect utilized, the mechanism of action always starts with a transfer of energy carried by the light beam to the tissue. We usually distinguish four effects (see Figure 7.1):

1. The thermal effect: energy is transformed locally into heat;
2. The photoablative effect: energy absorbed by the tissue causes the rupture of a certain number of molecular bonds;
3. The photochemical effect: light energy is absorbed by an exogenous chemical agent rendered thus active and capable of inducing cytotoxic chemical reactions;
4. The electromechanical effect: energy is transported by very short light pulses which induce the formation of a plasma at the origin of a shock wave which leads to a mechanical disruption of the tissue structure.

7.1.2. *Photomechanical effect*

When an ultrashort laser pulse (ns and below) is focused on a target tissue, thereby creating high irradiances (of the order of 10^{10} to 10^{12} W/cm^2), it is possible to obtain locally intense electric fields (10^6 to 10^7 V/m) comparable with atomic or intramolecular fields. Such fields induce an electrical breakdown of the material of the target resulting in the formation

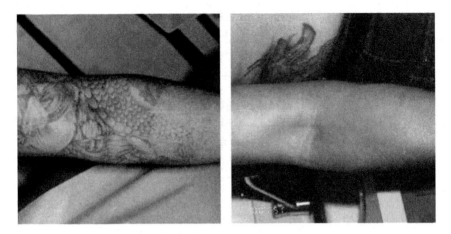

Figure 7.2:   Before and after tattoo removal achieved by a Q-switched Nd:YAG laser.

of a plasma. The shock wave associated with the expansion of the plasma generates extremely significant pressure waves and therefore a mechanical disruption of the tissue structure. This photomechanical effect is generally obtained with Nd:YAG lasers operating in Q-switched mode (ns) or mode-locked mode (ps). It is used in ophthalmology to destroy membranules of the eye that occur in particular after the implantation of an artificial crystalline lens. In dermatology, we turn to lasers operating in Q-switched mode (Ruby, Alexandrite, Nd:YAG) for the treatment of pigmented lesions and removal of tattoos (Figure 7.2). In the latter case, the large molecules of pigment (well tolerated by the skin) explode and give birth to smaller molecules which will be absorbed by the macrophages of the dermis. Furthermore, the explosion of microparticles of pigments generates micro-openings in the dermis contributing to the transepidermal elimination of part of pigment. Several sessions are generally necessary.

7.1.3.   Photoablative effect

The photoablative effect, also known as ablative photodecomposition, is based upon the use of photons having energy greater than the energy of the bonds of biological molecules. The photoablative process accordingly consists of a dissociation or a breakdown of the material and the ejection of fragments at supersonic speed. Photons having energy of the order of 3 to 5 eV are susceptible to dissociating peptide bonds or carbon–carbon bonds of polypeptide chains. Consequently lasers emitting in the UV such

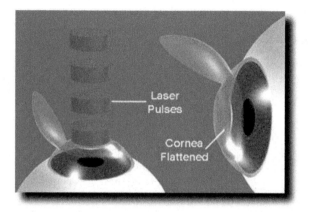

Figure 7.3: Principle of operation of LASIK.

as excimer lasers (ArF: 193 nm-6.4 eV or XeCl: 308 nm-4 eV) or even a frequency quadrupled Nd:YAG laser (266 nm-4.7 eV) are well suited for laser photoablation.

This effect is particularly used in ophthalmology for the refractive surgery of the cornea where it is possible to correct myopia, mild to moderate astigmatism, as well as small hyperopia. The Laser Assisted *In-Situ* Keratomileusis (LASIK) technique has progressively replaced photorefractive keratectomy (PRK) by laser, originally proposed. This technique (Figure 7.3) consists of using a microkeratome to cut a thin flap of cornea lifted temporarily, the time to proceed with the treatment of the corneal stroma. The membrane is then repositioned above the treated area and takes the new curvature of the cornea. The end of the first decade of this millennium saw the emergence of Intralasik where a femtosecond laser (see Chapter 4) now replaces the microkeratome.

7.1.4. Thermal effect

The thermal effect today constitutes the predominant mode of action for therapeutic applications of lasers. We will commence by presenting the successive mechanisms leading to tissue damage, and then we will give some examples of applications.

The thermal effect groups together a wide range of types of interaction characterized by a significant change of temperature inside the tissue illuminated by the laser. The thermal effect can also be achieved with either a laser exhibiting a continuous emission or with pulsed lasers. The thermal

Table 7.1:   Effect of temperature on the components of a tissue.

Temperature	Modifications
45°C	Vasodilatation, endothelial damage
50°C	Disappearance of enzymatic activity
60°C	Disruption of cell membranes Denaturation of proteins
70°C	Collagen denaturation Permeabilization of membranes
80°C	Shrinkage of collagen fibers Coagulation necrosis
100°C	Vaporization of water Total dehydration
>100°C	Volatilization of organic components

effect of lasers is a complex process consisting of three phenomena: a conversion of the laser light into heat (first stage), a transfer of heat into the tissue (second stage) and a tissue reaction dependent upon the temperature (third stage). Depending upon the duration of the heating carried out, and also as a function of the temperature rise of the tissue, we can obtain either a hyperthermia, a coagulation, or a volatilization of a given volume of tissue (Table 7.1).

There are numerous clinical applications, and this chapter does not allow us to detail them all. We will simply mention some representative indications. Ophthalmology and dermatology constitute the two principal applications. In ophthalmology, the prevention of retinal detachment by photocoagulation is one of the most practiced applications in the world (see Figure 7.4). The laser light (between 490 and 590 nm) is absorbed by the pigmented retinal epithelium rich in melanin and by the hemoglobin of the choroid. The thermal damage causes a denaturation of the proteins of the chorioretinal layers which results in a bleaching. The final result is a scar linking the retina, the epithelium and the superficial layers of the choroid.

In dermatology, applications are numerous and in 30 years indications have become refined and clarified. First purely medical: ablation of skin tumors with a CO_2 laser and treatment of flat angiomas with an Argon laser (see Figure 7.5). Lasers are now involved in the field of esthetics: treatment of aging skin with the CO_2 laser thanks to a superficial abrasion, treatment of redness and blotchy skin with a pulsed dye laser or a KTP laser, of acne with a mid-infrared laser.

Figure 7.4: Principle of treatment of the periphery of the retina during a detachment.

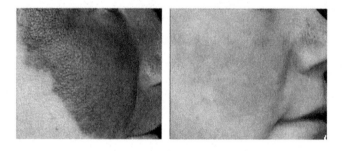

Figure 7.5: Treatment of a flat angioma with a pulsed dye laser.

Since 2000, one has also used the diode laser (810 or 980 nm) in phlebology, for the treatment of varicose veins. The endovenous laser (EVL) is then an alternative to the traditional surgery which consists of removing the saphenous vein. In this case, the fiber conducting the laser light is inserted up to the groin via a small incision into the vein to be treated (see Figure 7.6). The practitioner withdraws progressively the fiber whilst activating the laser in order to destroy the wall of the vein. This procedure takes a few minutes and the patient can then walk away one hour afterwards.

Laser interstitial thermotherapy was proposed several years ago to treat different cancerous lesions. The combination of modern imaging techniques, in particular MRI, allows us to precisely locate the tumor but also to determine first of all the path, and equally to calculate the exact position of one or several of the lasers fibers (1 mm in diameter) to insert. Laser interstitial thermotherapy in stereotactical neurosurgery is today proposed as a new alternative in the therapeutic treatment of certain brain tumors (see Figure 7.7). Thanks to MRI-guidance, it is possible to treat metastases of

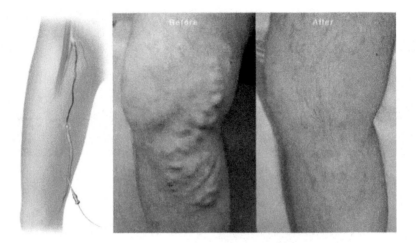

Figure 7.6:   Principle of endovenous laser treatment (EVLT). Results before–after.

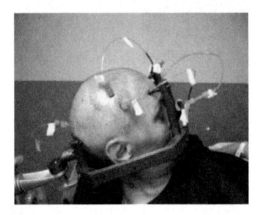

Figure 7.7:   Treatment by laser interstitial thermotherapy under the control of MRI calorimetry in real time. One sees here the intracerebral implantation of three optical fibers achieved under local anesthesia (image from Carpentier).

the liver. Finally, recently, prostate cancer (see Figure 7.8) could also be treated this way.

A new application concerns wound healing (see Figure 7.9) where recent data were able to show that by using thermal lasers, it became possible to modify the healing process to obtain a quasi-process of regeneration of the wound. In this case, we can use either a pulsed dye laser or an 800 nm diode

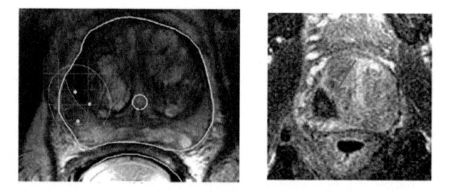

Figure 7.8: Treatment of prostate cancer by laser interstitial thermotherapy. To the left: MRI of the prostate (light edge) before treatment. This image allows us to define the optimal position of the fibers (dark edge) for treatment. To the right: necrosis (arrow) obtained seven days after the treatment.

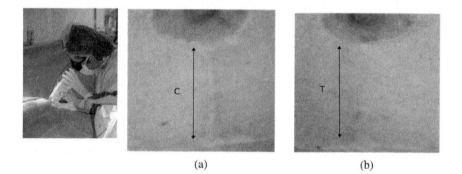

(a)   (b)

Figure 7.9: Treatment by an 810 nm diode laser (technique LASH). Breast — vertical scar belonging to a 35 year-old woman: (a) right breast untreated; (b) left breast treated by laser (result at 12 months). The treated part (T) and control part (C) are indicated. The laser had been applied along the incision immediately after suture (T) with a fluence of 110 J/cm^2.

laser which has the advantage of being portable (600 g) and therefore more practical to use in the surgical unit.

7.1.5. *Photodynamic effect*

Photodynamic therapy, commonly referred to using the acronym PDT, is the destruction of diseased tissue by a photochemical reaction. The principle is to label a pathological tissue with an exogenous chemical agent (photosensitizer), then to illuminate it with light of an appropriate wavelength in order to induce a cascade of photochemical reactions leading to the destruction of the treated lesion. The method is based upon a two-step process: (i) firstly, the application or injection of a photosensitizer or of a substance inducing the production of this photosensitizer allows us to achieve an accumulation of the latter in the zone to be treated; (ii) then illumination of this area is performed with a light whose wavelength is absorbed by the photosensitizer. The therapeutic effect is obtained by illumination at low irradiances (tens of mW/cm^2) and long durations (up to 10 minutes), without a thermal effect, allowing the activation of the photosensitizer and the production of cytotoxic compounds in the presence of oxygen. We speak of a photodynamic effect.

Several drugs are currently available on the market depending upon the indications and medical disciplines (see Table 7.2), other molecules are under development and are subject to clinical assessments.

The principal field of application for photodynamic therapy is oncology. Photosensitizers accumulate preferentially in neoplastic tissues which allow a priori a selective destruction of the tumor. However, the difference in concentration between healthy and tumoral tissue is often low and the selectivity is achieved primarily by the confinement of the illumination to the tumoral area. One observes also a high retention of photosensitizer in a number of healthy organs such as the liver, spleen, kidneys and, to a lesser extent, the skin. The slow elimination of the photosensitizer from skin tissue is at the origin of the major side effect of photodynamic therapy in the case of systemic administration, the skin photosensitivity of the patient. The elimination period is variable, from a few tens of hours to several weeks

Table 7.2:   Photosensitizers having medical agreement.

Molecule	Commercial name	Manufacturer	Excitation wavelength (nm)	Application
Hematoporphyrin	Photofrin® Photobarr®	Axcan Pharma	630	Gastroenterology Pulmonology
Meta-tetra Hydroxyphenyl chlorin	Foscan®	Biolitec	652	Gastroenterology Pulmonology
Benzoporphyrine	Visudyne®	Novartis	690	Ophtalmology
Bacteriopheophorbides	Tookad®	Steba-Biotech	753	Urology
Methyl aminolevulinate	Metvixia®	Galderma	570 to 670	Dermatology

after the injection of the product depending on the photosensitizer used. This problem does not arise for a topical application of photosensitizer, as in the case of dermatology.

The indications of PDT in oncology are multiple: palliative treatment of advanced cancer and tracheobronchial or esophageal obstruction, curative treatment of small cancers in these locations and cholangiocarcinoma. PDT can also be applied to precancerous lesions such as secondary dysplasia of the lower esophagus to an esophagitis by gastroesophageal reflux.

In dermatology, current indications, where the photosensitizer, derived from aminolevulinic acid (ALA), is applied locally as a cream, concern actinic keratosis and basal cell carcinomas (BCC); the results are comparable with classical techniques with superior cosmetic results. Photodynamic therapy is a highly advantageous replacement for surgical excision. Figure 7.10 shows one example in the case of actinic keratosis. In this case, topical 5-aminolaevulinic acid (ALA) is used to generate protoporphyrin IX (PpIX) in the skin whose fluorescence can be seen in the middle picture of Figure 7.10.

Applications of PDT are not limited to cancer. The technique is used in ophthalmology for the treatment of age-related macular degeneration (AMD). This pathology is the first cause of blindness in people over 65 years in developed countries. AMD in its exudative form is characterized by the formation of leaky choroidal blood vessels which grow under and through the pigmented epithelium of the macula causing its destruction and ultimately a loss of central vision. Photodynamic therapy is used here for its vascular action: it can close the choroidal neo-vessels by thrombosis without damaging the photoreceptors and the normal retinal vascularization.

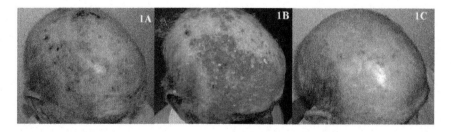

Figure 7.10:   Multiple actinic keratosis treated with methyl aminolevulinate photodynamic therapy. A: Prior to treatment. B: Illumination with violet light. The red fluorescence of protoporphyrin IX (PpIX) accumulated in actinic keratosis is clearly seen. C: Results after a single photodynamic therapy session.

The treatment involves injecting Visudyne® intravenously and illuminating the area of the neo-vessels at a wavelength of 689 nm, a few minutes after injection. Unfortunately, treatment has a limited effectiveness over time and must be renewed often, at an interval of few months.

The future of PDT should be assured by the development of new molecules with rapid clearance and more specific targeting, the availability of dedicated light sources and light diffusers appropriate for each application.

7.2. Laser Medical Imaging

7.2.1. *Introduction*

The first question that is legitimate to ask is: why using optics? Medical imaging uses, in fact, a wide range of methods (X-ray scanner, Magnetic Resonance Imaging, Ultrasound, Positron Emission Tomography, Nuclear Imaging) that are today well established in many hospitals at least in technologically developed countries. We have to acknowledge that the optical contrast clearly brings its own specific information: the color (spectrum), the texture (tissue morphology), as they appear to the eye of the surgeon or the pathologist, have a real diagnostic value; moreover the optical setups are often inexpensive (compared to the methods we have mentioned except perhaps ultrasound) and efficient (it is possible to focus a laser beam below 1 μm spot diameter and detect single photons).

The difficulty of the optical imaging of organs (here we will exclude cell imaging closer to biology than to medicine) comes from the strong light scattering by the tissues of the body that makes it difficult to access deep structures. Absorption behaves differently and remains low in the spectral region between 0.6 and 1.3 μm. The two images in Section 7.11 illustrate these two effects: the red light passes through the tissue because it is not absorbed by the blood, contrary to green or blue light. But it carries no information on the structures traversed because of multiple scattering.

Scattering decreases when using the infrared spectral region but we are limited by absorption of light by the water retained in the tissues. This limits the penetration depth of light.

Nowadays, lasers, thanks to their high spatial and temporal coherence and the ultrashort pulses that can be generated, make possible to revisit the field of medical optical imaging.

7.2.2. Which photons should we collect to form an image?

Before answering this question, let us first give a few orders of magnitude: the mean free path of photons (distance between two collisions with scatterers such as cells, nuclei or smaller structures) in tissues is about 50 to 100 μm. It is this figure, together with absorption, that defines the damping of ballistic photons (those that have not undergone collisions). This shows that at a few mm depth these ballistic photons have completely disappeared. However, in depths of the order of 1 mm, selection of the ballistic photons can allow forming images of high quality such as those we obtain in homogeneous media.

Another feature of scattering of tissue is the coefficient of anisotropy of the collision: the corresponding parameter is the average value of the cosine of the scattering angle. Its value is often large in tissues (0.8 to 0.95), which means that the diffusion is much more likely to occur in the forward direction. Therefore, typically 10 collisions are necessary to enter the multiple scattering regime for which laws are the same as for the heat diffusion or the dynamics of charged carriers in a semiconductor.

At larger depths (larger than 1 mm), lack of ballistic photons requires to work with multiply scattered photons: if one has a sufficiently narrow time gate, one can select the so-called "snake-like" photons that have followed a trajectory not too far from the ballistic one. When such selection is difficult, one has to work with all the multiply scattered photons that can be collected (see Figure 7.12).

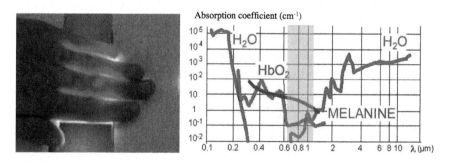

Figure 7.11: Scattering and absorption of light by tissues. In the left picture, no internal structure of the fingers can be seen because of scattering. In the right picture, the grey region in the red/near infrared spectral region corresponds to a relatively small absorption spectral domain in which light can travel through the tissues.

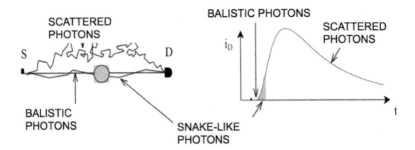

Figure 7.12: Schematic representation of the different classes of photons that can be used for medical imaging. In the left figure, a source S emits an ultrashort pulse. Ballistic photons reach detector D first without deviating from their initial trajectory, followed by snake-like photons and finally by all the multiply-scattered photons. The square represents the object (e.g., a tumor) one wishes to discover by imagery. The right figure represents the signal received by the detector versus time t.

7.2.3. Selecting ballistic photons using optical coherence tomography (OCT)

The principle of this imaging method, which is now widely established in the ophthalmology hospitals, is based on the fact that the broader the light source spectrum (either a continuous broad source or a pulsed femtosecond laser) the more precisely the interference phenomena (fringes) will be located in the vicinity of the zero path difference (see Section 7.13). The setup uses a Michelson interferometer illuminated by such a broad spectrum source. The interferences between the light reflected by the reference mirror and the light backscattered by the sample are localized in the vicinity of the zero path length difference. One thus obtains a signal originating from a well-defined depth inside the sample, that one can vary by sweeping the length of the reference arm of the interferometer. This principle of operation allows one to obtain real sections through the sample.

The best images could be obtained with lasers emitting pulses of a few femtosecond duration. But these lasers are still expensive and commercial apparatus use "superluminescent" diodes: these cheaper emitters combine the power and spatial coherence of laser diodes and the broad spectrum of LEDs, which is of the order of a few tens of nm.

Figure 7.14 illustrates one of the most routine applications of OCT: examination of the retina. On the left, one can distinguish a traditional image of the fundus with a green arrow that indicates the virtual section

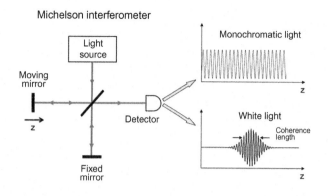

Figure 7.13: A monochromatic light source such as a single frequency laser generates interference fringes for all values of the path length difference between the two arms of the interferometer. With a broadband source (ultrashort laser, super luminescent diode, white light) fringes will be only localized around the zero path difference of each partially reflecting mirror: the principle of OCT is based on this physical phenomenon. In this figure, for the sake of simplicity, the interferometer is closed by a fixed mirror. For medical applications, the backscattering tissue plays the role of the fixed mirror.

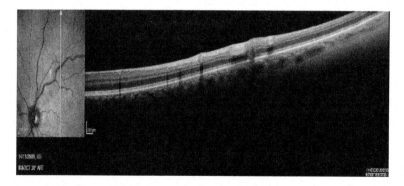

Figure 7.14: Examination of the retina by OCT. Left picture: traditional image of the eye fundus showing the network of blood vessels. Right picture: OCT depth image obtained along the green arrow of the left figure, for a 1 mm thickness. The different tissues of the retina can be distinguished. (Picture Pr. Michel Pâques, Hôpital des XV–XX, Paris, France.)

that will be performed by the OCT scan. One can see on the right side of the figure this virtual sectioning image. This examination of the retina by OCT is applied to multiple diseases: diabetes (thickness control, risk of detachment), macular degeneration, glaucoma, etc.

In its initial version, the OCT systems used moving mirror Michelson interferometers for scanning depth and a galvanometer mirror for lateral scanning. More recently, the coupling with a spectrometer led to the so-called Fourier domain OCT. The idea here is that each depth in the sample volume provides a wavelength modulated spectrum with a well-defined frequency. Another strategy consists in using a laser whose frequency can be quickly swept (swept source OCT). These strategies contribute to improve the performances of OCT.

The eye, with the retina and the cornea is, as we have said earlier, the privileged domain of OCT. In fact, the tissues of the eye are not "highly scattering" but rather "low backscatters" and OCT is used here to create "virtual sections" at different depths.

The two other areas where OCT starts to play a major role are: pathology, particularly with the aid to intraoperative diagnosis (i.e., real-time diagnosis during surgery), and dermatology.

Surgical specimens of tissues are highly scattering and assisting surgeons (tumor margins, sentinel lymph node status, ...) requires to operate with both large fields (of the order of $1\,cm^2$) and a resolution approaching that of a microscope, which is the working tool of pathologists, i.e., of the order of $1\,\mu m$. To date, only "full field OCT" achieves this resolution in the three dimensions of space: it uses microscopic interferometry coupled with spectrally broad light sources.

Figure 7.15 shows "virtual" sections of healthy and cancerous colon tissue obtained in a few minutes thanks to OCT, without preparation, and their comparison with histopathological sections that require a long preparation, which can take several days. One can easily see the breakdown of cancerous tissues structures when zooming in on a particular area.

To conclude, OCT provides a fast and cheap imaging method which exhibits a resolution at least 10 times better than ultrasound echography used for skin and eye imaging. In about 10 years only, this method has entered hospitals and its fields of application are rapidly growing.

7.2.4. Diffuse tomography

When ballistic photons can no longer be used, for example at depths exceeding a few tens of mean free paths, one enters the so-called "diffusive regime". One can imagine the difficulties of such an approach by looking at Figure 7.16, which represents the density of photons per unit volume between a source and a detector in a particularly simple geometry. These

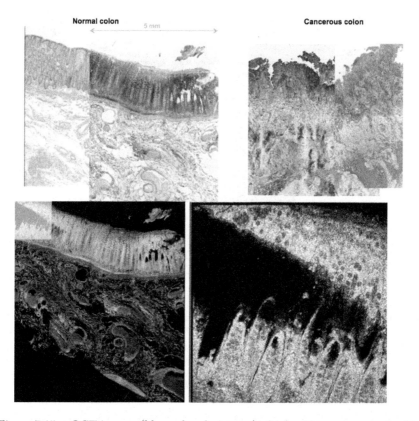

Figure 7.15: OCT images (blue-colored pictures) of colon tissue, compared with histology (red-colored pictures). Healthy tissues are on the left and cancerous tissues are on the right. Bottom pictures: zoom of the OCT image of a region of interest. The upper left corner of the lower left image corresponds to an enlargement of one part of the image. Images from LLtech (http://www.lltech.fr/).

pseudo trajectories in the diffusion regime are of course much more difficult to use for imaging purposes than the ballistic trajectories, which occur, for example, when X-ray imaging is performed. Just like in X-ray tomography where different series of signals corresponding to different positions of the source and detector are recorded and combined, a number of such "banana" shaped trajectories are usually combined between a set of sources coupled to a set of detectors. In order to reveal the spatial distribution of optical properties of the probed body, for example to detect a tumor, such tomography methods then require to solve a mathematical problem known as an "inverse problem".

SOURCE

DETECTOR

Figure 7.16: Banana-like photon trajectories in the diffusion regime. The false colors represent the volume density of photons between a light source and a detector. This density represents all the possible trajectories from the source to the detector. One clearly sees that most photons do not follow a straight line but rather obey a diffusive regime similar to heat propagation.

The two areas in which diffuse tomography is mainly used are breast cancer detection and brain activation.

Figure 7.17 reproduces the images of two breasts, one of which is diagnosed with a tumor and the other is healthy. The contrast here is associated with the change in absorption due to local angiogenesis. While the tumor localization reached by this method is good, it is so far not possible to study tumors whose size is well below $1 \, cm^3$. The reason for this is that here one needs to solve an inverse problem which is called an "ill-posed" problem particularly sensitive to boundary conditions. Moreover, the volume explored here is not only highly diffusing but also highly heterogeneous (presence of fat, supporting tissues, ducts, etc.).

The study on brain activation is now widely used in neurosciences: the spectacular images of MRI are probably the most common illustration, but electro-encephalography or magneto-encephalography are also used for the same purpose. Activation induces a significant influx of blood in the activated region, being itself a function of the performed task: complex motor task, reading, games, scrolling images, etc. This variation in the flow of blood induces a local variation of the absorption that is monitored

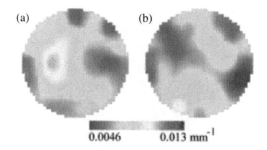

0.0046   0.013 mm^{-1}

Figure 7.17: Optical tomography of breast tumors. The left picture clearly evidences a big tumor inside the breast, detected thanks to its large absorption. The right picture corresponds to a healthy breast. The scale represents the absorption coefficient, which is linked to the vascularization (Optical tomography of the breast using a multi-channel time-resolved imager, Tara Yates, Jeremy C. Hebden, Adam Gibson, Nick Everdell, Simon R. Arridge and Michael Douek, *Phys. Med. Biol.* **50**, 2503–2517 (2005), with permission).

by optical tomography. The absorption spectrum analysis reveals not only the presence of blood, but also its oxygenation level because the spectra of oxidized and reduced hemoglobin are different in the near infrared region.

The advantage of using an optical device here is to avoid the use of heavy, expensive, and cumbersome equipment, such as a noisy MRI or SQUIDS requiring a magnetically shielded room. These rather light optical assemblies are now used by many laboratories and are subject to projects like video game interfaces (Figure 7.18). The idea here is that the monitoring of the localization and the intensity of the brain activation, which are associated with a decision being taken, could replace the manual control.

7.2.5. *Coupling optics and acoustics*

Whatever the future progress in the equipment or in the resolution of inverse problems solutions, optical tomography is very unlikely to reach a resolution much better than one-half of the depth that one wishes to explore. For breast, this leads to be able to observe details of the order of 1 cm, which is by far not good enough for an early diagnosis.

By coupling the optical signals with an acoustic localization, we are able to reveal optical contrasts with acoustic resolution (less than 1 mm).

The purpose of acousto-optic imaging is to "tag" certain areas of the sample with ultrasound. The block diagram of this method is shown in

Figure 7.18: From Hitachi, specialist and pioneer in diffuse tomography for brain imaging. Hitachi is considering the use of optical tracking of brain activity as an interface for video games. The optical fibers that can be seen in the figure are connected to detectors or sources allowing to perform the tomography of the brain activity. Such signals can be used to communicate with a disabled patient, to control a computer or video games (Hitachi, press release, 2007).

Figure 7.19: the sample is illuminated by a laser with a long coherence length. The wavelets that are emerging from the tissue have experienced tortuous paths in the scattering medium, thus generating a "speckle" pattern (linked to the random distribution of amplitude and phase). The ultrasonic wave modulates the phase of the light waves because it periodically compresses and expands the tissue. That is to say that in the regions of the tissue where the (scattered) optical field overlaps the (ballistic) ultrasonic field there is a path-induced difference at the ultrasonic frequency. The speckle is thus modulated at the ultrasound frequency and this modulation is specifically associated with the localization of the acoustic wave. For instance, if this zone is strongly absorbing, less tagged photons will emerge from it and the acoustically modulated signal will be reduced. By scanning the position of the acoustic wave, one can image the local optical properties of the probed medium and build images corresponding for example to an absorption contrast (see Figure 7.20). In this figure, acousto-optic imaging reveals two 3-mm-diameter absorbing spheres separated by 3 mm. They can be seen in the section of the sample on the right picture of Figure 7.20. The image on the left of this figure has been obtained by scanning the region shone by the ultrasound wave and shows the amplitude of the signal in a plane containing the two spheres.

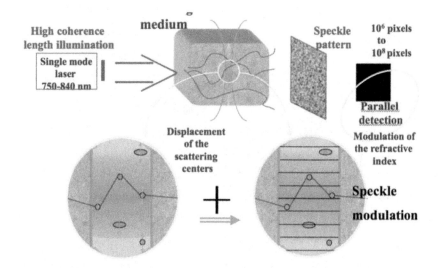

Figure 7.19: The modification of the optical path by acousto-optic effect in the scattering medium has two origins: the movement of the scatterers and the variation of the index of refraction induced by the compression and expansion. Because of the strong diffusion, light fills up the sample volume but only the photons that go through the zone shone by the acoustic wave are tagged by the ultrasound. This is equivalent to a virtual source of light modulated at the frequency of the ultrasounds, which can be scanned to form a 3D image of the optical properties of the probed body.

A different approach of hybrid acoustic/optical imaging is based on the photoacoustic effect (sometimes called opto-acoustic or thermo-acoustic effect). In this procedure, the sample is irradiated with light pulses (typically in the nanosecond range). This light diffuses into the depth of the probed tissue. The light selectively absorbed by the tissue structures produces a local heating (e.g., because of the vascularity around a tumor or when an absorbing selective contrast agent was injected). The rapid expansion following this heating creates a pressure wave whose spatial and temporal characteristics are related to the distribution of the absorbing zones. This wave propagates in all directions at the speed of sound in the medium (about 1500 m/s in tissues). It is detected, for example, by an array of ultrasonic transducers such as the standard arrays used in ultrasonic imaging. The localization problem is then simplified because from these absorbing zones ultrasound can propagate ballistically.

Lihong Wang and colleagues in Saint Louis (USA) have carried out images of the brain activity of rats or mice. Although many attempts have

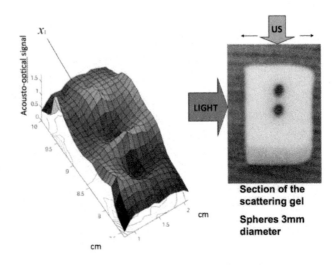

Figure 7.20:   Detection by acousto-optic effect of inclusions in an absorbing and scattering medium. A scattering gel sample was sectioned to reveal the absorbing zones (right image): when the ultrasonic pulse reaches this zone there are less tagged photons that are created and one can observe a decrease of the acousto-optic signal there (left image).

been made on breast imaging, photoacoustic imaging seems promising especially for imaging small animals (Figure 7.21), or for analysis of superficial signals such as vascularization of the skin, situations where the thickness of the organ is small.

7.2.6.   *From morphological to functional images*

Apart from monitoring the brain activity, as discussed in the examples above, most of the optical imaging techniques reveal a morphologic image at different scales of the body based on optical contrasts (scattering and absorption).

It is possible to use light to add more information to these morphological aspects, e.g., the frequency shift induced by the Doppler effect associated with blood circulation is important information carried by light.

The Doppler effect can be detected in the two regimes that we have described above:

The Doppler effect shifts the OCT signal in frequency. However, to reach the blood flow velocity one needs to access the morphological information that provides the angle between the direction of the probe beam and the blood vessel axis (Figure 7.22).

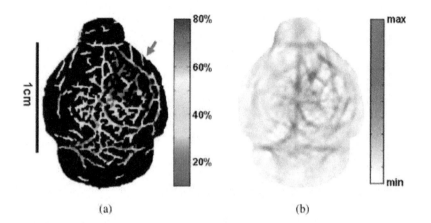

(a)   (b)

Figure 7.21: Functional and molecular photo-acoustic imaging. The photo-acoustic signal (left image, *in vivo*) reveals the different absorption levels between oxidized and reduced hemoglobin in the region of the tumor. This result is confirmed by the histopathology (right figure, obtained *ex vivo*) (labs.seas.wustl.edu/bme/Wang/image_gallery.html, with permission).

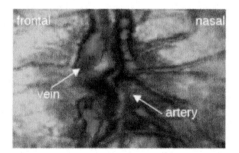

Figure 7.22: The OCT signal, due to backscattered light, is frequency shifted by the Doppler effect induced by the movement of red blood cells in the blood flow. The false colors code the sign of the Doppler effect: the flow in the veins is reversed with respect to the arteries. The saturation of the colors represents the velocity of the blood flow (Resonant Doppler flow imaging and optical vivisection of retinal blood vessels, A. H. Bachmann, M. L. Villiger, C. Blatter, T. Lasser and R. A. Leitgeb, *Optics Express* **15**(2), 408–422 (2007), with permission.)

In the multiple scattering regime, the Doppler effect does not occur as a simple shift of the frequency of the probe light but through a broadening of the spectrum of the backscattered light. This effect is utilized to analyze *in vivo* blood flows in the rat brain, as can be seen in Figure 7.23.

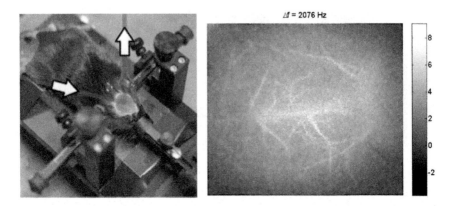

Figure 7.23: *In vivo* observation of the Doppler effect in multiple scattering regime. Here, the photons that interact with the moving red blood cells have random directions. The Doppler effect then manifests itself by a spectrum broadening that depends on the velocity of the blood flow. The signals associated with the speed of various vascular blood flows are selected by analyzing the frequency distribution: at high frequency, about 2000 Hz, the associated blood flow signal clearly differs from the background of the brain (Cortical blood flow assessment with frequency-domain laser Doppler microscopy, Michael Atlan, Benoît C. Forget, Albert C. Boccara, Tania Vitalis, Armelle Rancillac, Andrew K. Dunn and Michel Gross, *Journal of Biomedical Optics* **12**(2), 024019 (2007), with permission).

7.2.7. *Conclusion*

We have tried to illustrate through these examples a few breakthroughs in optical imaging applied to medical diagnosis. It is a field still open to new investigations. It is strongly multidisciplinary and the expectations are placed very high: we must do better, i.e., for example faster, cheaper, with new types of contrasts, than existing techniques, and convince the medical world of the merits of a new approach.

The laser is once again at the center of new approaches, which are always more efficient, less expensive, more compact. It is associated with the progress of optoelectronics for detection purposes. We can be optimistic regarding the future of this topic.

Finally, the association of spatial light modulators (SLM) and single-frequency or short-pulse lasers has recently demonstrated imaging through scattering media. We anticipate that such techniques will open the path to new valuable biomedical imaging approaches.

Chapter 8

All the Things This Book does not Mention

The laser has much more applications, either industrial or scientific, than what the 170 pages of this book can contain. We have thus performed a selection, and many subjects have not been dealt with in spite of the fact that they are as fascinating as the ones described here.

First, the field of nonlinear optics has only been mentioned here and there. This domain was born thanks to the availability of lasers that provide the necessary intensity. Nonlinear optical effects permit to generate new frequencies, not directly reachable by lasers, as shown by the ubiquitous green laser pointer. They also provide many scientific and industrial probing techniques.

Then, many direct applications of lasers, such as, e.g., laser alignment of buildings, laser printing, laser cutting, laser surface processing, laser welding and marking, laser cleaning of art pieces, have hardly been mentioned. The same thing is true for the laser probing of gas traces in the atmosphere or, more generally, the physical and/or chemical laser analysis techniques applied to many different domains. The laser has also triggered many new developments in biology (such as, e.g., nonlinear optical imaging techniques) or in chemistry (femtochemistry is an example).

The laser has also induced the development of many new technologies such as new optical coatings permitting to tailor the properties of optical components, new semiconductor growth or processing technologies to design new light sources, detectors, or components. It has also revolutionized material sciences in the domain of optical glasses and crystals, either linear or nonlinear.

Of course, the laser has also many military applications for guidance, telemetry, designation, counter-measures,...that we have hardly mentioned.

Obviously, the laser is also the source of many discoveries in scientific research. Mentioning only physics, it is for example at the origin of all the developments in quantum information science or in the wide domain of coherent control of physical processes.

But the most amazing applications of lasers are those that are still to be discovered. Consequently, very dear reader, it is up to you now!

Index

CPSIA information can be obtained
at www.ICGtesting.com
Printed in the USA
LVOW02s1442240316

480597LV00007B/53/P